Obedience

THE BIBLICAL KEY TO HAPPINESS

F. B. HUEY, JR.

BROADMAN PRESS
NASHVILLE, TENNESSEE

©Copyright 1990 ● Broadman Press

All rights reserved

4254-52

ISBN: 0-8054-5452-7

Dewey Decimal Classification: 248.4

Subject Heading: OBEDIENCE

Library of Congress Card Catalog Number: 89-48736

Printed in the United States of America

Unless otherwise stated, all Scripture quotations are from the Holy Bible, *New International Version*, copyright ©1973, 1978, 1984 by International Bible Society.

All Scripture quotations marked KVJ are from the King James Version of the Bible.

All Scripture quotations marked RSV are from the *Revised Standard Version of the Bible*, copyrighted 1946, 1952, ©1971, 1973.

Scripture quotations marked Williams are from the *Williams New Testament, The New Testament in the Language of the People*, by Charles B. Williams. Copyright ©1937, 1966, 1986 by Holman Bible Publishers. Used by permission.

Scripture quotations marked NASB are from the *New American Standard Bible.* © The Lockman Foundation 1960, 1962, 1963, 1968, 1971, 1972, 1975, 1977. Used by permission.

Library of Congress Cataloging-in-Publication Data

Huey, F. B., 1925-
    Obedience : the biblical key to happiness / F.B. Huey, Jr.
        p.   cm.
    ISBN: 0-8054-5452-7 :
    1. Happiness--Religious aspects--Christianity. 2. Obedience-
    -Religious aspects--Christianity. I. Title.
    BV4647.J68H84 1990
    234' .6--dc20

                                                                        89-48736
                                                                        CIP

To my wife Nonna
and our children
Mary Anne, Linda, and David,
my constant reminders that
blessed is the man who trusts in the Lord (Ps. 84:12).

Contents

1
Is There a Secret for Happiness?

Teenage suicide, broken marriages, a drug epidemic, violence, terrorism, senseless murders, aborted babies, child abuse, fears of financial catastrophe, and always the specter of nuclear disaster—not the picture of a happy people!

What's wrong in paradise? Who would try to make a case for us as a happy people, basking in our affluence and role of *primus inter pares* (first among equals) in world affairs?

We cannot be faulted for not trying to be happy. In fact, a large part of our time, energies, and resources are devoted to a frantic pursuit of happiness. If the money spent on all forms of entertainment could be totaled—such as travel, sports, the arts, parties, eating out, movies, TV, reading, and stimulants ranging from caffeine to illegal drugs—the pursuit of happiness would be our number-one industry.

Obviously, something is wrong. We ought to be the happiest people on earth. We have the resources. We have the intelligence. We have even put men on the moon. We surely devote enough time to finding happiness. "Heaven" for many people in the Third World nations is immigrating to the United States, legally or illegally. But if a poll were taken in our "paradise," millions would reply, "I'm not really happy."

The more frantically we search for happiness, the more elusive it becomes. We buy books, attend seminars, and frequent health studios, but we never seem to find that magical formula which will bring instantaneous happiness.

The search for happiness is not a phenomenon of the twentieth century arising from the complexities and uncertainties of our fast-moving age. Its origin goes all the way back to the first man and woman in the garden of Eden. They bought the tempting suggestion that they could find happiness by becoming like God, if they would only disobey Him. Paradise could have been theirs forever by obeying God in one small matter—not eating the fruit of just one tree in the garden. But it was forfeited in an instant by their disobedience (Gen. 3).

Though some historians may refuse to acknowledge the theological implications of human history, the story of the human race from that time to this has been the story of an effort to regain paradise by disobedience, that is, by living on our terms rather than on God's.

Warfare, which has occupied the major time and resources of human history, is based on a belief that one nation (or at least the leaders who foment wars) can be happy by controlling or by forcibly taking the land, resources, or people of another nation. But no war has ever brought genuine, lasting happiness. The only lesson we seem to learn from history is that we learn no lessons from history!

Some dream of returning to a simpler way of life as the means of discovering happiness. They believe that our ancestors, lacking the conveniences of modern civilization, must have been blissful. This "back-to-nature" idealism can only be called naivete or wishful thinking. The establishment of a commune in a remote region somewhere in the Rocky Mountains will not bring happiness. The abandonment of supermarkets and department stores to raise our own food and make our own clothes will not restore Eden. Giving up the conveniences of water from a faucet and of sewage facilities in order to draw water from a well and make a daily trek to an outhouse won't do it either!

Primitive man may have concluded momentarily that happiness could come through the discovery of fire or the wheel. The bow and arrow replaced the club, and that, in turn, was replaced by gunpowder, but these "improvements" didn't usher in the golden age, either. Nor did the airplane, automobile, or television. Certainly the nuclear age, with undreamed of energy available for all humanity, has not brought happiness.

The ancient Greek myth of King Midas is a reminder of the centuries-old dream of achieving happiness through wealth. Midas wished that all he touched would turn to gold. His wish was granted, but he nearly starved to death because even the food and drink he touched turned to gold. Midas pleaded with the gods to take away the power that he had foolishly thought would bring happiness.

Alchemy was based on the belief that a substance could be found that would turn base metals into gold and silver. It originated in ancient Egypt. Alchemy had an unbroken history of adherents for the next thousand years, climaxing in Western Europe during the thirteenth through the fifteenth century, with many "scientists" devoting their careers to finding the magic ingredient that would produce gold. They overlooked the fact that if other substances could be easily turned into gold, the precious metal would have become as worthless as rocks that could be picked up from the ground. Alchemy was only another manifestation of the effort to find happiness through acquiring wealth by one means or another.

The possession of youthful vigor and health as the key to happiness has for centuries had its advocates. Health studios and athletics are not a late twentieth-century invention. The Irish had their organized sports, the Tailteann games or Lugnasad, about 2500 years ago. The Greeks had their gymnasiums (although the Greek philosophers and physicians were almost unanimous in condemning athletics as injurious not only to the mind but also to the body!). Rome had its Actian games established by Emperor Augustus.

In merry old England, young men of good families were taught to run, leap, wrestle, joust, and perhaps rescue a young maiden in distress now and then! During the reign of Henry VIII, the sons of noblemen were advised to give themselves to sports and leave study and learning to the sons of the lower classes.

Vigorous exercise, however, may not be the panacea for what ails us, contrary to the claims of its advocates. Many physicians today are saying that being happy contributes more to good health than any exercise or diet program. They are confirming what a wise man stated hundreds of years ago: "A cheerful heart is good medicine" (Prov. 17:22).

Ponce de Leon, the Spanish governor of Puerto Rico, abandoned his administrative responsibilities in 1513 and set out in search of the land of "Bimini," where, according to an Indian legend, there was a fountain with water that would restore youth. Ponce de Leon never found the magic fountain but in the process of his search discovered what we now call Florida. Perhaps some of the thousands of retirees who flock to Florida every year believe they will discover their lost youth there!

Christians are not immune to the lure of discovering the magic ingredient that will give instant happiness. Witness the success of books that have become Christian classics, such as Hannah Whitall Smith's *The Christian's Secret of a Happy Life*, first published in 1870 and still in print. In 1899 Charles Sheldon wrote *In His Steps* that was a bestseller for years. The underlying message of Sheldon's book is that we would be happy if we would always ask "What would Jesus do?" before we speak or act. His message was on target—we would be happy if we obeyed Christ in everything that we do. But the principle was too demanding for most; the book finally lost its appeal, and the search continued for an easier way to find happiness.

Dale Carnegie's *How to Win Friends and Influence People* appeared in 1936. It sold millions of copies and is still in print (quite a feat, as any author would attest!). Why the book's phenomenal appeal? Bluntly stated, Carnegie was suggesting (perhaps subliminally) that happiness can be achieved by making friends in order to manipulate them for one's benefit.

Carnegie tapped a gold mine with the discovery that millions of people would like to have a simple set of rules for being happy.

Ten years late in 1946, Joshua Loth Liebman produced a runaway best-seller, *Peace of Mind,* by combining the most attractive aspects of popular psychology and religion in order to achieve happiness (which Liebman called "peace of mind"). Obviously, the thirst for books on how to find happiness had not yet been quenched.

With the success of these books, the floodgates were opened in the 1950s. Writers and publishers discovered an insatiable market of millions of people who would buy any book that claimed a magical formula (painless and easy, of course) which would bring instant and permanent happiness.

In more recent years publishers have found a sure market for books that promise happiness through losing weight by some kind of miracle diet. Books on sex are guaranteed to sell because of the widespread belief that happiness can be achieved through sexual gratification.

Both religious and secular writers have profited from the ongoing fascination with finding happiness, but the fact that books on the subject appear with monotonous regularity serves as a reminder that perhaps the elusive "magic formula" remains to be isolated.

In the 1960s and 1970s a frightening new twist in the search for happiness surfaced among the under-twenty-five generation. To the surprise of their elders (who thought that just being under twenty-five was sufficient grounds for happiness), a generation announced its discontent and unhappiness in vocal and sometimes violent ways. It claimed to discover a new shortcut to happiness (not found in books, for it was a generation that was not reading!). Some called it flower power or love power although most who were proclaiming it looked desperately confused and unhappy. In its more violent forms it seemed to say, "Love is the answer, even if we have to throw rocks and burn buildings to demonstrate our love." It quickly embraced its discovery of what it proclaimed as a new shortcut to happiness: LSD, marijuana, cocaine, and whatever other mind-numbing drugs were available.

The message seemed to be that happiness could be found by ceasing to think or by living on feelings alone or, as some of its disciples said, "Freak out. Do whatever makes you feel good." The new route to happiness could not deliver what it promised; instead, it wrecked untold numbers of lives. Yet the drug culture is still growing by dangerous leaps and bounds, revealing our national desperation to find happiness, even at the risk of destroying ourselves.

It's depressing. Throughout our history, we have consistently failed to find the one thing we want most--happiness. The more frantically we search, the more elusive the goal becomes. But just as we never give up believing politicians' promises during election year, so we continue the search for happiness and are quick to flock to the latest guru who claims to have the secret (at a price, of course!).

The frenzy of trying to find happiness reminds me of an experience on a summer vacation to California when our children were small. Our then nine-year-old son, David, saw his first mirage on a stretch of highway through the Arizona desert. From the back seat of the car, standing and peering over my shoulder, David watched with fascination the shimmering lake of water that always seemed to be a bit further down the highway. Finally, he could contain his excitement no longer and shouted, "Daddy, drive faster so we can catch up with it!"

Is happiness, after all, a mirage that is always going to be just out of our grasp, however frantically we seek it? Or is it possible to be really happy? Is there actually a "secret," a "key" that will unlock the door into the Elysian fields of bliss, where fear, frustration, worry, and unhappiness no longer exist?

I believe there is such a "secret." It would be arrogant, presumptuous, and dishonest to label it as my personal discovery. The secret is really not new, but too seldom has it been applied. The purpose of this book, then, is to share with you what some have already discovered as an unfailing way to be happy, even in the midst of unhappy circumstances.

A part of the problem in discovering happiness is the difficulty of defining exactly what happiness really is. If we don't know what we are looking for, we will not likely find it! Imagine if you came home some day to discover your spouse or child frantically pulling clothes out of every drawer and dragging boxes out of closets to examine their contents. You would assume that he or she was searching for something quite important. But if you asked, "What are you looking for?" and got the reply, "I don't know, but I'm just looking!" you would have just reason for concern. Doesn't that describe the way most people are going about looking for happiness? They really don't have a clear picture of what happiness is. No wonder they search for it in so many ways and in so many places but never find it.

The "secret" to happiness that I want to share s is not easy to apply, but it works. If you have tried other ways to happiness, only to find that they fail, I invite you to be open to God's "secret" for being happy.

2
Obedience as the Gateway to Happiness

There is a verse in the Bible that ought to be very disturbing to Christians: "We demolish arguments and every pretension that sets itself up against the knowledge of God, and we take captive every thought to make it obedient to Christ" (2 Cor. 10:5).

Does the verse trouble you just a little bit? It should. Consider its profound challenge for the Christian. It states unmistakably that the chief goal for the Christian is not a halfhearted submission to the teachings of Christ. Rather, our goal should be total acquiescence, even making every thought obedient that passes fleetingly through the shadows of the mind. The apostle Paul was using the image of a captive, enslaved, bound, and completely subjugated to the will of his master, combined with the picture of one who has submitted willingly to captivity.

Paul understood the awesome influence of thoughts and that all our actions begin first with the thought. What we think about will eventually determine what we do (Matt. 15:16-20). Whatever or whoever controls our thoughts will also control what we do. If our thoughts are dominated by Christ, then our actions will be, also. If our thoughts are dominated by evil, what we do will also be evil. The most terrible catastrophe in human history, World War II, that resulted in the killing of more than fifty-five million people around the world began in the mind of one man in the 1920s: Adolph Hitler.

The Discovery of a Vital Truth

Sometimes we discover the most important truths quite by chance. My awareness of the centrality of obedience for the Christian life came about unexpectedly as I was reading the autobiography of Helen Keller.[1] The book contained a letter written by Anne Sullivan to a friend in 1886 shortly after coming to the Keller home to be the teacher of Helen, then age six. The letter revealed the key to Miss Sullivan's remarkable success as the teacher of a very unpromising pupil.

Helen Keller's life is one of the great inspirational stories of this century. Although stricken with an illness at nineteen months that left her completely blind and deaf, Helen became one of the most famous and beloved persons in the world. In spite of seemingly insurmountable limitations, she had a captivating personality and a mind so alert and stimulating that great and famous people from all parts of the world counted it an honor to be her friend. Yet she lived all the years of her life in total silence and darkness.

Helen Keller showed none of the characteristics of the gracious person the world came to know when Anne Sullivan first came to the Keller home as Helen's teacher. Living in her world of silence and darkness, Helen was uncontrollable and rebellious. She reacted like a frightened, helpless bird in a cage frantically beating against its bars trying to escape. She was living in her prison of blindness and silence, separated from human love and friendship.

Anne Sullivan wrote a letter to a friend, describing one of her first efforts to break through the barriers. It involved an attempt to teach table manners to Helen. The letter spoke for itself:

> I had a battle royal with Helen this morning. . . . Helen's manners are appalling. She puts her hands in our plates and helps herself, and when the dishes are passed, she grabs them and takes out whatever she wants. This morning I would not let her put her hand in my plate. She persisted, and a contest of wills followed. Naturally the family was much disturbed, and left the room. I locked the dining-room door, and proceeded to eat my breakfast, though the food almost choked me. Helen was lying on the floor, kicking and screaming and trying to pull my chair from under me. She kept this up for half an hour, then she got up to see what I was doing. I let her see that I was eating, but did not let her put her hand in the plate. She pinched me, and I slapped her every time she did it. Then she went all around the table to see who was there, and finding no one but me, she seemed bewildered. After a few minutes she came back to her place and began to eat her breakfast with her fingers. I gave her a spoon, which she threw on the floor. I forced her out of the

chair and made her pick it up. Finally I succeeded in getting her back in her chair again, and held the spoon in her hand, compelling her to take up the food with it and put it in her mouth. In a few minutes she yielded and finished her breakfast peaceably. Then we had another tussle over folding her napkin. When she had finished, she threw it on the floor and ran toward the door. Finding it locked, she began to kick and scream all over again. It was another hour before I succeeded in getting her napkin folded. . . . I . . . went up to my room and threw myself on the bed exhausted. I had a good cry and felt better. I suppose I shall have many such battles with the little woman before she learns the only two essential things I can teach her, obedience and love.[2]

In another letter she wrote:

I saw clearly that it was useless to try to teach her language or anything else until she learned to obey me. I have thought about it a great deal, and the more I think, the more certain I am that obedience is the gateway through which knowledge, yes, and love, too, enter the mind of the child.[3]

My first reaction after reading the last sentence was that Anne Sullivan had confused the order of her words. I was certain that what she meant to say was, "Love is the gateway through which obedience and knowledge enter the mind of the child." However, I could not forget her words, and I began a serious study of the biblical teachings on obedience. I became convinced that she expressed a profound truth. It is one that is applicable for all of us, not just for a handicapped child over 100 years ago.

I examined Miss Sullivan's statement and related it to many statements in the Bible regarding obedience. As a result I have become firmly convinced that obedience is a neglected biblical emphasis in practice, though we may affirm the principle. Truly, obedience is the gateway through which knowledge and love—knowledge of God and love for Him and others—enter the mind, not only of the child, but also of all of us. It is the key to happiness.

Though none of us would deny the biblical emphasis on obedience, many of us do not take it seriously. Rebellion has become the *in* word during the past two decades. It expresses itself in art, literature, motion pictures, and the moral revolution that began in the 1960s. *Obey* is probably the most unpopular word in the English language today.

Rarely is it heard in marriage ceremonies or anywhere else. No one wants to be told that he or she *must* do anything!

Even sincere Christians, if completely honest, have to admit that the word *obedience* irritates us slightly. It is easy to respond that we are saved by faith through grace and not by buckling under some irksome demands of a crotchety God. Didn't Paul say, "Are you so foolish? After beginning with the Spirit, are you now trying to attain your goal by human effort? . . . Clearly no one is justified before God by the law" (Gal. 3:3,11)?

It is not too difficult to conclude that somehow faith and obedience are on a collision course, and one must give way to the other. There is a popular notion that people in Old Testament times were saved by obeying certain laws, especially those involving animal sacrifice, but for the Christian everything is of faith. Actually, in Old Testament times, people were also saved by their faith (Gen. 15:6; Rom. 4:3,5,9-12; Heb. 11).

The Old Testament contains numerous commands regarding sacrifices and offerings. However, the prophets reminded the people, "To obey is better than sacrifice" (1 Sam. 15:22). Isaiah told them God did not delight in their sacrifices because of their disobedience (Isa. 1:10-20). Micah exhorted the people that walking humbly with God was better than bringing thousands of rams or ten thousands of rivers of oil (Mic. 6:7-8).

Amos told them that God hated their feasts but wanted justice to roll down like rivers of waters (Amos 5:21-24). God spoke unequivocally through Jeremiah: "Obey me, and I will be your God" (Jer. 7:23). Jeremiah also reminded them that they could not break God's moral laws and expect God's protection (Jer. 7:8-11). Malachi called on the people to bring their tithes if they wished to experience God's blessings (Mal. 3:10). But his appeal should not be misinterpreted to mean that *only* bringing the tithe was sufficient to ensure God's blessings, whether the moral laws were obeyed or not.

If the laws of sacrifice did not secure a relationship with God, what, then, was their purpose? Keeping the laws, whether sacrificial or moral, was an expression of the people's faith. It was as though they were saying, "God told us to keep these commands. Because we believe God, we will show our faith by obeying His commands."

We will respond in one of several ways when someone asks us to do something. We may refuse in order to show our disdain for that person or because we think the request is not in our best interest. We may do it out of fear of retaliation or harm which that person can do us. Or we may do it because we want to please that person to demonstrate our respect and friendship, or because we perceive it as beneficial to us. The same motives will determine how we respond to God's demands.

The Old Testament Emphasis on Obedience

There is no doubt that the Old Testament emphasizes obedience. Words such as *obey, keep,* and *observe* are found more than 500 times in the Old Testament. The obedience emphasis can be summarized by the appeal: obey, and you will be blessed. Disobey, and you will be cursed (see Deut. 11:27-28; 28:1-68).

The ancient Israelites' understanding of obedience is revealed by their use of the same Hebrew word to mean either "hear" or "obey." For the Israelite, to hear the command of God was not a passive experience. It required a total response of obedience to the command. He did not require psychological or theological explanations in order to understand obedience.

If we shut our ears and refuse to allow God to speak to us through His Word, through a dedicated friend, or by some other means, according to the ancient Israelites, we are being disobedient.

An illustration will clarify the point. Do you remember those times as a child when you were doing something you thoroughly enjoyed? Invariably, it seemed those were the moments your parent called you to do something that would interrupt your play. Parents never seem to call when the child has nothing else to do! If you were outdoors or in the next room, sometimes you responded not too loudly, "Uh-huh," and continued playing. You reasoned that if the parent thought you did not hear, you were under no obligation to answer. You quickly learned, however, to recognize the tone of voice (usually the third call) beyond which you dared not risk further refusal to respond. You had pretended not to hear because you did not want to obey.

The Israelites understood that when God spoke, obedience was the expected response. Like us, however, they did not always obey. Deuteronomy 6:4-9 is called the Shema by Jewish people because its first word, *shema*, is the Hebrew word *hear*. "Hear, O Israel" could also be translated "Obey, O Israel" because the same word has both meanings. Even our English word *obedience* (from the Latin *ob* + *audire* = to hear) suggests the link between hearing and obeying.

If Anne Sullivan was right that obedience is the gateway by which knowledge and love enter our lives, we can better understand why obedience is given such emphasis in the Old Testament. It has frequently been stated that Israel was in a "kindergarten" stage of relationship with God at Mount Sinai. During their years of slavery in Egypt, many of them forgot the God of Abraham, Isaac, and Jacob and worshiped the gods of Egypt (see Josh. 24:14; Ezek. 20:8; 23:3).

At Sinai they were coming to know God again and learning what they could expect of Him and what He could expect of them. Therefore, it was necessary for Him to deal with them as children. Parents usually say to very small children, "Do this," or, "Don't do that." Only later when the child is able to understand do the parents add explanations to their commands.

Hosea 11:3 describes a father patiently teaching his child to take its first steps: "It was I who taught Ephraim to walk." Israel was like a child not ready for a complete revelation of God at Sinai. That was reserved for "the fulness of the time" (Gal. 4:4, KJV; Heb.1:1-2).

How does a child learn? Teachers know that learning must begin on the simplest leveland become more demanding as the student builds on what has been learned previously. Math students do not begin with advanced calculus or trigonometry. Mathematical knowledge begins on the simplest level of learning that "two plus two equals four," etc. Learning to read begins with the alphabet and "See Spot run," not with the *Encyclopedia Britannica*.

Teachers also know that the child who listens carefully to instructions and then attempts to carry them out learns more rapidly than the child who is indifferent or refuses to obey the instructions.

In the early school years, a child is introduced to the multiplication tables. The teacher says that they must be repeated over and over until they are learned. So the tedious process begins: "Two times two equals four; two times three equals six, . . ." However, suppose the child rebels, crosses his or her arms defiantly, and says, "I will not learn the multiplication tables." The kindest thing we could say is that such a child will not likely become a great mathematician!

In like manner God knew that the Israelites could learn more readily about Him if they would hear His commands and obey them. By commanding: "You shall not kill," God was revealing to them the sacredness of human life. By commanding: "You shall not commit adultery," He was teaching them the sanctity of the marriage relationship. God did not give them a 200-page theological and philosophical discussion to explain why He did not want them to kill or commit adultery.

New Testament Emphasis on Obedience

The emphasis on obedience in the Old Testament is indisputable, but of what interest is that to Christians who claim to be under a New Covenant rather than Old Testament laws? It may surprise some to discover how frequently obedience is also stressed in the New Testament. The fact that grace has replaced law does not mean that disobedience has replaced obedience!

Jesus did not say that He had come to abolish the law and to exempt us from obeying God's commands. He came to fill the law full of new meaning (Matt. 5:17), as revealed in His reinterpretation of certain Mosaic laws (see Matt. 5:21-48). Jesus summarized all the requirements of the law in two simple commands: love God supremely, and love others as yourself (Matt. 22:37,39). One of the scribes agreed with Jesus that loving God and our neighbor is more important than all burnt offerings and sacrifices (Mark 12:33).

Love is an outstanding New Testament emphasis, but it is also emphasized in the Old Testament. The statement is frequently made that God is a God of wrath in the Old Testament, whereas He is a God of love in the New Testament. Shibboleths like this reveal fuzzy thinking. God's love is also emphasized in the Old Testament—recall Hosea and many Psalms. His wrath is equally emphasized in the New Testament—recall Matthew 23—24 and the Book of Revelation. We dare not be schizophrenic in our concept of God and assume that a wrathful God somehow got "converted" and became a loving God. He is the same yesterday, today, and forever (Heb. 13:8). Law and love do not need to be set against each other as antagonists.

In the New Testament love was intentionally linked to obedience by Jesus on a number of occasions: "Not everyone who says to me, 'Lord, Lord,' will enter the kingdom of heaven, but only he who does the will of my father who is in heaven" (Matt. 7:21). "Whoever has my commands and obeys them, he is the one who loves me" (John 14:21). "If anyone loves me, he will obey my teaching" (John 14:23). "This is my command: Love each other" (John 15:17). "This is love for God: to obey his commands" (1 John 5:3). Our desire to obey God should be just as spontaneous and joyful as our love for Him.

Difficulties with Obedience

Some people seem to have no difficulty understanding and explaining every verse in the Bible. I am not in that charmed circle! I am still struggling to understand verses like Philippians 2:8:

> And being found in appearance as a man,
>   he humbled himself
> and became obedient to death—
>   even death on a cross.

Did the perfect Son of God struggle to submit to death? Did He have the freedom to disobey (like Adam and like you and me)? Could He have rejected the cross at the last minute? Hebrews 5:8 reminds us that Jesus "learned obedience" through His suffering. Was He not already perfectly obedient? What did He have to learn that He did not already know? I will leave the answers to questions like these to more erudite minds!

Though we may never fully understand verses like Philippians 2:8 and Heb. 5:8, we do know that it was His obedience that will make many righteous (Rom. 5:19). Whatever else we may or may not understand about Philippians 2:8, it is significant that the two words *humility* and *obedience* are joined in the same statement. It reminds us that obedience, whether human or divine, requires denial of self: "Not my will, but yours be done" (Luke 22:42).

If we are completely honest with ourselves, we must admit that total obedience, even including our thoughts, is the most difficult biblical doctrine to put into practice. Why? The only answer is that it is not easy to humble ourselves! Christians can preach, give the tithe, sacrifice in many ways, go to the mission field, and even die for the faith, without being humble. How many of us will come to the end of this life and be able to say truthfully: "I took 'captive every thought to make it obedient to Christ' "? We talk about total surrender, but it is easier to preach than to practice!

The Long History of Disobedience

Obedience is not a problem peculiar to this generation. Every generation has faced it, for we are all rebels against God by nature. The disobedience of the first man and woman brought sin and death into the world (Rom. 5:12). They could not understand why God demanded total obedience about a matter so trivial as the fruit of one tree in Eden. If they could eat the fruit of the other trees, why not that one, also? The more Eve thought about it, the more the restriction irritated her. She must have concluded that God was not just in requiring such strict obedience, and it was not difficult to convince her husband, too.

As a male I find it difficult to accept Phyllis Trible's interpretation of the temptation story of Genesis 3. Truth usually hurts! Trible pointed out that the narrative is careful to tell us that the man was with his wife (Gen. 3:6). Furthermore, all the verbs used by the serpent in the preceding dialogue (Gen. 3:1-5) are plural: the devil was speaking to both of them. Trible continued:

> Throughout this scene the man has remained silent; he does not speak for obedience. His presence is passive and bland. . . . No patriarchal figure making decisions for his family, he follows his woman without question or comment. . . . the story . . . does not present him as reluctant or hesitating. He does not theologize; he does not contemplate; and he does not envision the full possibilities of the occasion. Instead, his one act is belly-oriented, and it is an act of acquiescence, not of initiative. If the woman is intelligent, sensitive, and ingenious, the man is passive, brutish, and inept.[4]

As males we like to take comfort in 1 Timothy 2:14: "Adam was not the one deceived; it was the woman who was deceived and became a sinner." However, Paul's words may be expressing criticism, not justification, of the male. True, Adam was not deceived. Instead, he accepted the forbidden fruit with his eyes wide open, knowing that what he did was wrong!

Why did he not refuse the fruit and also insist that Eve not eat it? I think the answer is the same answer given by many men when confronted with temptation. Adam's desire to please the woman and receive her approval was greater than his desire to please God. Samson made a similar decision when pressed by Delilah to reveal the secret of his strength (Judg. 16:15-20).

When we put God's will first, we cannot make a mistake. When we put others ahead of God, our disobedience can only bring unhappiness and separation from God (Gen. 3:23-24). However we may explain Adam's role in the temptation experience, we need to remember that Romans 5:12-14 explicitly says Adam sinned, and Genesis 3:17-19 describes his punishment for listening to his wife.

The pleasure promised by the tempter for disobeying God was short-lived. Disobedience always brings loss, punishment, and alienation from God. The title of a sermon preached hundreds of times by the renowned Baptist pulpiteer R. G. Lee, "Pay Day Some Day," sums up the consequences of disobedience to God's commands.

Why Can't We Obey God?

Why is it so difficult to obey God? He never requires anything of us that is not in our best interest or that would be hurtful to us. Jesus said, "My yoke is easy and my burden is light" (Matt. 11:30). The only answer I can give is that we are by nature self-centered. It is difficult to abdicate the throne of self and permit God to take His rightful place as our Lord and Master. We prefer to insist,

I am the master of my fate;
I am the captain of my soul.[5]

Submission to another person is contrary to our nature. We want to be in control and the masters of our destinies. However, the apostle Paul reminded us that the person who thinks he is lord because this position has been denied to God is not really his own master but the slave of sin. We are either servants of righteousness or of sin (Rom. 6:14-23; see 2 Pet. 2:19). No one is really his or her own master. The only freedom we have is choice of masters. The paradox of the Christian faith is that only by submitting to the lordship of Christ do we become truly free (John 8:32,36).

Principle: Obedience is God's way to true happiness.

Notes

1. Helen Keller, *The Story of My Life* (1902; reprint, New York: Dell Publishing Co., 1961).

2. Ibid., 263-64.

3. Ibid., 265.

4. Phyllis Trible, *God and the Rhetoric of Sexuality: Overtures to Biblical Theology* (Philadelphia: Fortress Press, 1978), 113.

5. William Ernest Henley, "Invictus," *The Literature of England: An Anthology and a History,* vol. 2, 3d ed., eds. George B. Woods, Homer A. Watt, and George K. Anderson (Chicago: Scott Foresman and Co., 1948), 866.

3
Obedience Applied to Life's Problems

Any hypothesis, if it is to be taken seriously, must be subjected to practical testing. If my belief that obedience is the biblical key to finding true happiness is valid, we should be able to apply it to problems which cause our unhappiness. We will discover that obedience to biblical teachings enables us to deal with the problems and thus alleviate the source of our unhappiness.

Obedience and Suffering

One of life's greatest mysteries and the source of countless questions is human suffering, especially that of a devout Christian. Though we can never fully understand Hebrews 5:8, it does say that we should not expect better treatment from a hostile world than our Lord received. The servant is not greater than his master (Matt. 10:24). We cannot expect to be exempt from experiencing suffering, but as Christians we do have One who is with us *in* the suffering.

Some of us cannot learn true obedience except through suffering, whether physical, mental, or spiritual. Some respond to misfortune by angry defiance of God, putting the blame on Him, although humankind is the source of all sin and evil. Others respond with trustful submission to the suffering. The obedience produced by that submission may be the gateway through which a better knowledge of God is gained. Our love for Him is also strengthened, and even the suffering becomes bearable. When that happens, we are able to conclude that our trials can be the means of spiritual growth. Some of the most radiant, inspiring people are those who have experienced the most pain and suffering.

A young friend called me recently to share his grief that his wife had been diagnosed as having Hodgkin's disease. The disease was spreading so rapidly the physicians determined that the child she was carrying should be taken immediately by Caesarean section. They gave no hope for her recovery. Faced with this Joblike calamity of the loss of his wife and raising a child who would never know his mother, my friend's voice trembled as he said, "I 'know that all things work together for good to them that love God' " (Rom. 8:28, KJV).

Job's faith enabled him to say, "Though he slay me, yet will I hope in him" (Job 13:15). Habakkuk affirmed that even if everything were taken away, he would rejoice in the Lord:

> Though the fig tree does not bud
> and there are no grapes on the vines,
> though the olive crop fails
> and the fields produce no food,
> though there are no sheep in the pen
> and no cattle in the stalls,
> yet I will rejoice in the Lord,
> I will be joyful in God my Savior (3:17-18).

These verses remind us that our faith should not depend on favorable circumstances of the moment. Genuine faith is secure because it is "in-spite-of" faith. A response of trustful submission in time of suffering or crisis may not provide ready answers, but it will be more help than angry accusations hurled at God.

A profound understanding of the necessity of submission in the midst of painful, inexplicable situations was expressed by a most remarkable French woman, Madame Jeanne Guyon, around 1685:

I introduce a new word to you. The word is abandonment. To penetrate deeper in the experience of Jesus Christ, it is required that you begin to abandon your whole existence, giving it up to God. Let us take the daily occurrences of life as an illustration. You must utterly believe that the circumstances of your life, that is, every minute of your life, as well as the whole course of your life—anything, yes, everything that happens—have all come to you by His will and by His permission. You must utterly believe that everything that has happened to you is from God and is exactly what you need.[1]

Madame Guyon was put in the infamous Bastille for nine years for writing the book that contained these words and other books like it.

Obedience and the Family

Obedience to God's commands has something to say to today's stressful and often shattered family life. Many, if not most, of the difficulties of today's families stem from not accepting our individual responsibilities in family relationships that are stated in the New Testament. The husband ought to love his wife as Christ loved the church (Eph. 5:25)—unselfishly, sacrificially, and faithfully. The wife should be submissive to her husband (Eph. 5:22; Titus 2:5). Husband and wife should be submissive to each other (Eph. 5:21), that is, they should be sensitive to meeting each other's needs. Children should be obedient to parents (Eph. 6:1), but parents should not be unreasonable with their children (Eph. 6:4).

If every member of the family obeyed these biblical principles, family problems would largely disappear. Home would become a little bit of heaven on earth! Our nation of broken homes, unwanted children, violence, drugs, and suicide is reaping the bitter fruit of disintegrated family relations.

Obedience and the Church

The church could also learn from the biblical emphasis on obedience. Many people have shut out the church from their lives. They accuse it of being irrelevant to life's problems and uncaring. They say its members are hypocritical in their life-styles and that it only wants people's money. These accusations would not stand up if the church really were the church our Lord intended it to be. But it can only be the true church by obeying our Lord's teachings.

There are churches which deny the authority and reliability of the Scriptures. They deny that miracles did or could take place and reject Jesus' claim to be the only "way, the truth, and the life" (John 14:6, KJV). An insistence on obeying God's commands where there is no confidence in the Scriptures would not be taken seriously. Such a stance is often disobedience wearing the mask of relevance. On the other hand there are churches that insist on the utter trustworthiness and authority of the Scriptures, but their members sometimes seem less concerned about obeying the Scriptures than defending them. These members may demonstrate an intolerant, unloving spirit toward anyone who disagrees with them. When such is the case, disobedience wears the mask of orthodoxy. Frankly, if each of us took the call to obedience more seriously, the church's witness would be better served.

Jesus left a command (not a request) for the church. He said, "Go and make disciples of all nations" (Matt. 28:19). It is a command that is largely ignored by the church today. One reason for the failure to evangelize has been the failure of the home to teach obedience to children! A well-known evangelist of many years experience stated that it is very difficult to win people to Christ who were not taught to obey at home when they were children. If a person cannot respect his or her earthly parents, how much more difficult it will be to obey a Father in heaven who cannot be seen. And what about the child of a broken home who grows up without a father? As parents, we are preparing the way for the salvation of our children by teaching them the importance of obedience.

Obedience and the State

Obedience to the government is emphasized in the New Testament (Rom. 13:1-7). In an era when it seems that many government leaders are corrupt and insensitive to the will of the people, demanding more and more tax money to spend in irresponsible ways, it is difficult to maintain a submissive attitude. However, when Paul wrote Romans 13:1-7, Christians were under one of the most corrupt, cruel, and immoral governments the world has ever known.

Civilizations which have grown and prospered have been those that developed an elevated concept of law and order. When people lose respect for their own laws and refuse to obey them, or take the law into their own hands, the result has always been decadence and the eventual downfall of that civilization. Christians must find Christian ways to change government when it is not responsive to the best interests of the people.

Why the Biblical Emphasis on Obedience?

As rational people our first response when someone asks us to do something may be one of the following: "Why should I do this?" "Is this the best thing to do?" "Will it hurt or help me?" or, "What's in it for me?" The same questions occur when we try to explain the emphasis on obedience in the Bible.

Perhaps an analogy will provide a partial answer. If we willingly do something another person asks us to do, we demonstrate confidence in that person, whether we verbally express it or even think it. We do what that one asks because we are confident that person would never ask us to do something that would hurt us or not be in our best interest.

When we refuse to obey parents, a friend, someone in authority, or God Himself, we are saying that we really do not have confidence in that person. This principle is demonstrated in family relationships by observing that younger children often learn more rapidly than older brothers and sisters. Why? Because the younger have such perfect confidence in the older ones! They imitate the older ones because they believe that what they do is right and good.

An unforgettable family experience convinced me of the influence of older children on the younger. When our son David was age five, nothing would persuade him to eat spinach. No amount of coaxing would persuade him to taste it. Appeals that it tasted good, that it was healthy, and (the clincher in those days) that Popeye ate it fell on deaf ears! However, one day when we were having spinach, David's sister Mary Ann, seven years older, said, "Look David. I like spinach." She then preceded to eat it. David looked intently for a moment at her eating spinach and then at the spinach on his plate. Then without a word he picked up his fork and began eating his spinach!

Why did David have such confidence in his sister (on this occasion, even more than in his father!)? Because of the good relationship he enjoyed with his older sisters. They never tried to trick him, tease him, or get him in trouble, as some older siblings do. Therefore, he had absolute confidence in them. David knew he could trust his sister, even about spinach!

The Bible appeals to us to be like obedient children (1 Pet. 1:14).

When we readily obey the commands of God, it is the surest evidence that we have confidence in Him. An unknown wise person once said, "Perfect obedience would be perfect happiness if only we had perfect confidence in the power we were obeying."[2]

The Transforming Power of Obedience

Human logic says that to obey someone else will result in the loss of personal liberty. However, we actually do not find true liberty except through obedience. I am not suggesting that Christians should become spineless creatures, politely saying to everyone, "Yes, Sir," or "No, Sir." There is a proper time and place for Christian rebellion—but not against God. We ought to rebel against the gutter morality that is being forced on us through the various media. We ought to rebel against the appeal that there are no absolutes of right or wrong, and, therefore, "I can do whatever makes me feel good." We ought to rebel against scoffers who deny that we are created in the image of God and insist that we are nothing more than animals, here for a senseless moment and then gone.

Christians must rebel, but against the world as it is. "We must obey God rather than men!" (Acts 5:29). Peter's statement is the spirit of true Christianity rebellion, which, paradoxically, is the spirit of true Christian obedience.

The image of Christ is formed in us when we obey, not when we disobey. The greatest difficulty Christians face is the subjugation of their wills, or as Paul expressed it, to "take captive every thought to make it obedient to Christ" (2 Cor. 10:5). Saul of Tarsus would probably have become a leading citizen among his people, but Saul would not have rated even a footnote in history if he had continued to rebel against the claims of Christ (Acts 9:2-4; 26:14). When he submitted to Christ's mastery, Saul became a great man, the apostle Paul, whose influence on all subsequent human history has been incalculable.

The early life of Helen Keller revealed a human personality unformed, savage, and uncultured, but which was transformed into a sensitive, beautiful, and well-educated person whose life became an inspiration to millions of people. What would have been the outcome if her teacher, Anne Sullivan, had failed in her efforts to teach obedience to the child? We would never have heard of Helen Keller, and the world would have been impoverished by not having known her.

If only we could be obedient disciples of Christ! If only we could surrender ourselves fully—even every thought and every desire to Christ. Then He could transform us so that our lives would make an impact for good on our world.

Obedience is truly the gateway through which knowledge of God and love for Him and for others enters our lives. The rebel, the non-conformist, and the one who refuses to submit to Christ never really find happiness. Only the person who accepts the invitation of Jesus finds it:

> Come to me, all you who are weary and burdened, and I will give you rest. Take my yoke upon you and learn from me, for I am gentle and humble in heart, and you will find rest for your souls. For my yoke is easy and my burden is light (Matt. 11:28-30).

Through obedience we find solutions to life's perplexing problems. When we put on His yoke of obedience, we at last find that elusive quality we call inner peace and happiness.

Principle: Total obedience to the commands of Christ in every area of life is the basis of all true happiness.

Notes

1. Jeanne Guyon, *Experiencing the Depths of Jesus Christ* (original title: *Short and Very Easy Method of Prayer which All Can Practice with the Greatest Facility, and Arrive in a Short Time, by Its Means, at a High Degree of Perfection,* ca. 1658; reprint, Goleta, Calif.: Christian Books, 1975), 32.

2. Quoted by Hanna Whithall Smith, *The Christian's Secret of a Happy Life* (1870; reprint, Westwood, N.J.: Fleming H. Revell Co., 1952), 208.

4

The Undivided Heart and Individual Happiness

Somewhere I read that for years Billy Graham has read five chapters in Psalms and one chapter in Proverbs each day. In this way he reads through each of these books in a month and then begins the cycle again. Several years ago I tried the plan.

I had reached the eighty-sixth Psalm one morning, but my attention was not focused on what I was reading. A thirty-five-year-old friend of mine in another state was undergoing open-heart surgery at the very hour. The condition had been discovered during a routine examination. The blockage was so advanced that surgery was ordered immediately.

My straying thoughts were jerked back to what I was reading when I noticed verse 11: "Give me an undivided heart." The coincidence of the word in the psalm with the heart surgery being performed at that moment led me to make an intensive study of the meaning of an "undivided heart."

I discovered that the Hebrew actually says, "Unite my heart" (the translation of the *King James Version,* the *Revised Standard Version,* and others). The Hebrew word means "to bring together." It could be used to describe the pieces of a jigsaw puzzle being put together to form a complete picture.

Teenagers sometimes say, "Get your act together." They mean that chaotic, senseless behavior should be replaced by orderly, reasonable conduct. In that sense Psalm 86:11 could be translated, "Get my heart together." Whether translated as "unite my heart" or "give me an undivided heart," this particular expression is found nowhere else in the Bible.

In the context of Psalm 86, David was in trouble. He had discovered that enemies were seeking to kill him. Fear gripped him, and he could not think clearly. He cried out to God for help. He pleaded for God to unite his anxious thoughts to fear God rather than his enemies.

Biblical Usage of the Word "Heart"

The heart is mentioned quite often in the Bible, altogether 858 times in the Old Testament and 158 times in the New Testament. The Hebrew word is *leb* or *lebab*. The Greek word is *kardia* (from which our word cardiac comes). In the Old Testament, the heart is mentioned in all but five of the thirty-nine books, most frequently in Psalms, Proverbs, and Jeremiah. The New Testament mentions the heart in all but five of its twenty-seven books, with no particular concentration in any of them.

A word in most languages can have multiple meanings. For example, I can say, "I love my wife," "I love pecan pie," or "I love to travel." Likewise, the word *heart* has many meanings in the Scriptures. Sometimes it is the literal organ in the chest, even as we use the word (2 Sam. 18:14; 2 Kings 9:24). It is sometimes used, as we do, to refer to the seat of the emotions—love, sadness, joy, etc. (1 Sam. 1:8; Prov. 14:30; 23:17; and John 16:22). Ordinarily, however, the intestines were considered by the Hebrews to be the seat of the emotions. If you have ever had an upset stomach, you can understand why they associated the stomach region with emotion!

Most of the time, the heart in the Bible is the equivalent of what we call the mind, the intellect, the understanding, or the will. It is the decision-making faculty of a person (Gen. 6:5; 1 Sam. 25:37; Prov. 6:18; 16:9; Mark 7:21; Luke 2:19; and 2 Cor. 9:7).[1]

Five times the Bible says animals have hearts (2 Sam. 17:10; Job 41:24, KJV; Hos. 7:11, KJV; and Dan. 4:16, KJV; 5:21, KJV). Twenty-six passages state that God has a heart (see 1 Sam. 2:35; 13:14). Most of the time, however, the word refers to the human heart.

Many adjectives, most of them in the Old Testament, are used to describe the heart. They include the following: broken (Ps. 51:17); hardened (Ex. 8:15; Mark 3:5); willing (Ex. 35:5); clean (Prov. 20:9); trembling (Deut. 28:65); merry (Ruth 3:7); wise (1 Kings 3:12); perfect (1 Chron. 28:9); soft (Job 23:16); understanding (Prov. 8:5); perverse (Prov. 12:8); proud (Prov. 21:4); heavy (Prov. 25:20); stony (Ezek. 11:19); pure (Ps. 24:4; 1 Tim. 1:5); wicked (Prov. 26:23); foolish (Rom. 1:21); evil (Heb. 3:12); good (Luke 8:15); and true (Heb. 10:22).[2]

A linguistic analysis of the word *heart* gives some insight into its biblical meaning. We can conclude that when David asked for an undivided heart, he was probably asking to be able to think clearly in a dangerous situation. He may have been asking God to calm the surge of emotions that were overwhelming him: fear, indecision, anxiety, foreboding, or pessimism.

Long before modern psychology had explored the mind, David understood that when our thoughts and emotions are fragmented and out of control, there is no inner peace or happiness. Helmut Thielicke observed in his book *The Waiting Father* that depression has its roots in a divided heart. He said, "Only the simple and the singlehearted are happy."[3] Only when our thoughts are brought into singleness of focus do we function as whole persons. There can be no true happiness when we have divided hearts. It is understandable then, that since David asked for an undivided heart, he was also asking God to make his soul glad (Ps. 86:4).

How to Recognize an Undivided Heart

Statistical and linguistic information about the biblical usage of the word *heart* may be interesting, but the more crucial question is: "How can I know whether my heart is undivided?" "What are the characteristics of the undivided heart?"

Freedom from a Spiritual Tug of War

I believe there are four tests we can use to discover if we have an "undivided heart." First, the undivided heart is free from the spiritual tug of war that can exhaust us physically and emotionally. The apostle Paul was experiencing an internal spiritual battle in Romans 7. He finally cried out, "For what I do is not the good I want to do; no, the evil I do not want to do—this I keep on doing. . . . What a wretched man I am! Who will rescue me from this body of death?" (vv. 19,24).

Elsewhere we are told that we cannot serve two masters (Matt. 6:24). We cannot maintain twin loyalties to two causes. James 1:8 says the double-minded person is unstable in everything he does. Many people go through life experiencing spiritual schizophrenia. Their life-styles are so changeable that sometimes it seems they are two different people. The inability to commit ourselves to undivided loyalty to Christ has earned Christians the reputation of being "Sunday Christians." We often compartmentalize our Christianity by reserving our pious behavior for Sunday and acting like the world the rest of the time.

There is no true happiness in indecision. It can be a time of anguish, depending on the importance of the decision to be made. Buying a house or a car can be a time of major indecision because of the financial obligation about to be assumed. Trying to decide which line to join at the supermarket or the bank can be a moment of lesser anxiety, but real, nevertheless! Have you ever stood for a moment at the check-out lines trying to decide which one is shorter and moving the fastest? That moment of indecision can be upsetting. However, if your experience is like mine, don't spend much time in making the decision. Whichever line you join will be the wrong one! Invariably just as I reach the front, there is a snag with the customer ahead of me. Either the cash register breaks down, or an article is not properly tagged and a clerk is sent to find the price, or there is some problem with the customer's identification which requires that the manager be called to approve the check.

Making selections while going through a cafeteria line can be another of those difficult decision-making times for some people, especially when they get to the dessert section. They first look at all the desserts, tentatively pick up one and put it back, trying to select the largest serving. Somehow as the customers move on down the line, they never look quite happy, still wondering if they made the right decision!

Indecisiveness at the checkout lines or the dessert counter can be one of life's minor moments of agony. The wrong decision there will not be life threatening, nor will it result in perpetual torment. But indecisiveness in spiritual matters can be devastating to peace of mind. The inability to make a firm decision to follow Christ at all costs is the major source of most people's unhappiness.

Priorities Are Settled

The second test of the undivided heart is that life's priorities have been settled. The Scriptures encourage us to determine our priorities: "Seek first his kingdom and his righteousness, and all these things will be given to you as well" (Matt. 6:33). "Love the Lord your God with all your heart and with all your soul and with all your mind and with all your strength" (Mark 12:30).

A commentary by a Jewish scholar on Psalm 86:11 said that the undivided heart is a heart that is entirely concentrated on God.[4] By that statement he did not mean that God expects us to think exclusively about Him from the moment we awake until we go to sleep. Rather, it expresses an attitude of life that gives primacy to God, not in thoughts alone, but in the way all of life is lived.

The undivided heart requires the kind of concentration required by a pilot landing a plane on the deck of an aircraft carrier. The daring and precision required in this maneuver is amazing. It always appeared so effortless in films I had seen that I never thought about the problems involved until I heard some pilots describe it. One pilot said that even with sophisticated communication equipment, just locating the carrier on the ocean and maneuvering the plane for a landing can be a task. He said that it is like sighting a pinball machine at the far end of a football field. Another said it is like finding a needle in a haystack and then trying to land the plane on that needle!

A World War II fighter pilot described to me the difficulty of landing on a carrier. He said that the plane is traveling at 120 miles per hour, the boat is moving forward, and the waves are rocking the carrier up and down. The pilot must take all these factors into consideration. If he loses his concentration for a fraction of a second and miscalculates a few feet below or above the target deck, the result will be disastrous.

The undivided heart does not lose its concentration on God because it has already settled life's priorities.

Consistency of Life

There is a third test that helps us know whether our heart is undivided. If our priorities are settled, and we are giving God first place, then the undivided heart is consistent in its actions. We are not pulled in a thousand directions so that our behavior becomes totally unpredictable. People can depend on us to be what we claim to be and to do what we say.

The consistent person is not like the preresurrection Peter. In one breath Peter could make the most exalted statement of faith to be found in the Scriptures: "You are the Christ, the Son of the living God" (Matt. 16:16). However, a few moments later Christ had to rebuke him for protesting His impending death: "Out of my sight, Satan! You are a stumbling block to me" (Matt. 16:23).

On another occasion Peter insisted that even if all the other disciples fell away, he never would (Matt. 26:33). But before that night ended, Peter had betrayed Jesus three times by denying he knew Him. Sometimes our own words of commitment prove to be just as unreliable as Peter's when we find ourselves in a tempting situation.

An inspiring Sunday evening service enjoyed by many churches is the time of testimonies shared by young people who have just returned from a week at Bible camp. The glow on their faces is contagious. Their testimonies, even when clumsily expressed, have such a ring of sincerity about them that they delight the congregation. Their proclaimed resolve to live consistently for Christ before their friends can bring tears of joy to the hearers.

I don't want to sound like a cynical Scrooge in the midst of such inspirational moments, but I confess I do not always share the rapture of those giving testimonies. Even as I am listening, I want to say, "Come back in a month, and if your testimony is still the same, I will join you in your excitement." I have seen the glow disappear all too often in just a few days after the youth groups "descend from the mountain" back into the real world of friends at school, peer pressures, and enticing temptations.

Our inconsistency of being on the mountaintop one moment and down in Carnal Valley the next has earned us the label "hypocrite" all too often.

The word *hypocrite* has an interesting history. It developed in the context of the Greek drama where a person played a role on the stage, pretending to be someone other than who he as. The players would hold a mask over their faces to indicate the mood they were conveying—a smiling mask for a happy face, a frowning mask for a sad face. In a moment the happy mask could be exchanged for a frowning mask. It was impossible to know the true feelings of the person behind the mask.

I have observed that people who claim to have no interest in Christianity are the first to blow the whistle on our inconsistencies. Though they may not accept our beliefs, they often know how Christians ought to live better than we do!

Because Christians all too often do not practice what they preach, a skeptical world finds it difficult to take us seriously. Probably the greatest barrier to accepting Christ by unbelievers is the gap between what we claim and what we live. It has been reported that Mahatma Gandhi, the powerful Indian leader whose ascetic life-style swayed millions of people, after reflecting on his earlier school years spent in England, said, "I might have become a Christian if I had ever met one!" What would have been the course of Indian history if Gandhi had returned to his own land as a Christian!

We ought to be able to say, "What you see is what you get!" I was intrigued to discover that the word *cosmetics* comes from a Greek word that means "to bring order out of chaos." Too many Christians practice cosmetic Christianity. They pretend a shallow outward piety to cover up the real person and are satisfied if the outward image deceives other people (even though God is not deceived).

I once noticed a photograph of the ugliest baboon I have ever seen hanging beside a small mirror on the wall of a pastor's study. Beneath it were printed the words, "Maybe my mistake has been trying to make it on looks." The Christian whose heart is undivided does not live an inconsistent, superficial life.

Obedience as Evidence of the Undivided Heart

This book is about obedience as the key to finding happiness. Obedience is the fourth and most accurate test to determine the undivided heart. This chapter has attempted to show that only the heart that is undivided experiences happiness. The connection between the two emphases ought to be obvious. The best evidence of the undivided heart is obedience to Christ's commands. A person can become a Christian in a few seconds, but living the Christian life requires a lifetime commitment of growing and learning.

The Old Testament prophets present striking contrasts in their levels of obedience. One of them, Jeremiah, had a major problem with obedience. From the moment God called him, Jeremiah protested that he was inadequate for the task assigned him (1:6). He questioned why God would allow wicked people to prosper (12:1). He could rejoice one moment and complain about his unceasing misery the next (15:16,18). He asked whether God was as unreliable as mountain streams whose waters fail in the heat of summer when most needed (15:18).

Jeremiah's lowest moment of alienation came when he decided he would no longer proclaim God's messages. He discovered that the messages were like fire burning in his bones, and he could not keep silent (20:9). He could exult, "Sing to the Lord! Give praise to the Lord!" in one breath (20:13), and in the next curse the day that he had been born (20:14).

By contrast, Ezekiel is an example of that rare person who seems to have no problem with obeying God. Ezekiel did whatever God asked him to do, even at the risk of ridicule or death. Once God told him to cut off all his hair and divide it into three piles. He was commanded to burn one pile, toss one in the air and slash at it with a sword, and throw the third pile into the wind to blow away (5:1-4). If you saw someone do that and then say, "The Lord told me to do it!" you would probably conclude he or she was insane. Ezekiel was not exempt from that same accusation, but his commitment to obey God enabled him to take the risk of lost reputation. His heart was undivided.

Why Should We Want an Undivided Heart?

Even if we can recognize an undivided heart, another question remains. Why should I want an undivided heart? Why did David ask God for an undivided heart when the immediate situation was a threat against his life? Psalm 86:11 not only contains David's appeal for an undivided heart. It also gives the reason for wanting it.

In the Hebrew language there is a preposition called the *lamed*. It sometimes functions as a *lamed* of purpose, sometimes as a *lamed* of result. In Psalm 86:11 it appears immediately after David's appeal for an undivided heart. If it expresses purpose, the rest of the verse could be translated: "*for the purpose of* fearing your name." If it expresses result, it should be translated: "*with the result that* I will fear your name." Either translation of the *lamed* would be correct in the context.

The more important question is: What does it mean to fear the name of the Lord? In the Old Testament *fear* can mean "dread" or "terror," as we would normally use the word. However, it can also be used with the meaning of obedience, reverence, submission, or worship. Thus, to fear the Lord can mean to obey, to revere, to submit, or to worship. David's request in 86:11 falls in this second category of meaning rather than the basic meaning: "dread" or "terror."

Still another question remains. Why does the verse say "fear your name" instead of "fear You" or "fear the Lord"? The expression "the name of the Lord" is found frequently in the Old Testament. In order to understand its significance, we have to understand what ancient peoples believed about names.

People in the ancient Near East, including the Israelites, believed that the name revealed the attributes or true character of a person. Names were carefully chosen because of a belief that the name could even influence the personality of the child. Though such a belief may seem strange to us, the eminent Swiss psychiatrist Paul Tournier in his book *The Naming of Persons* affirmed the validity of this belief. Tournier said an unusual name can affect the personality. It may embarrass the persons or make them look ridiculous in the eyes of society. He appealed to parents to use care in naming their children and to avoid unusual names because of the effect this can have on their personalities.[5] The technical name for the influence of names is metonomasia.

The name is so closely identified with the person that it represents everything that person is. For example, if I say, "Billy Graham," you immediately associate certain qualities with his name that identify the kind of person he is. If I say, "Adolph Hitler," you make a different set of associations with his name that identify his character. People who know you or me associate the qualities of your personality or mine immediately upon hearing our names.

The "name of the Lord," then, represents everything that God is, every quality that we attribute to Him. He is living, loving, merciful, patient, forgiving, eternal, righteous, all-knowing, all-powerful, and so forth.

Therefore, when David said he wanted an undivided heart so that he could fear the name of the Lord, David was saying that he wanted his commitment to be total and sincere and his allegiance to God to be unconditional. David wanted that kind of undivided loyalty so that he could worship God with full understanding of who God is.

If an undivided heart is necessary for obedience, and obedience is the gateway to happiness, then all of us should want an undivided heart.

How to Acquire an Undivided Heart

One question remains: How do we acquire an undivided heart? Once again, the verse itself answers our question. Notice that David addressed his appeal to the Lord: "Lord, . . . *give me* an undivided heart" (author's italics). The undivided heart is a gift of God. It cannot be bought or earned. It cannot be pretended.

If we sincerely want to be free from the inner conflict of loyalties that keeps us in turmoil, we can be. If we want to get our priorities right and focus on the things that are really important, we can. If we want to live consistent lives that will not bring embarrassment or shame to the name of Christ, we can. How? By yielding to God. By submissive obedience, we can replace a fragmented, shattered life with one of wholeness and purpose. Life is no longer a battlefield because peace has been made with God. If we want it, we can receive the gift of the undivided heart.

Principle: Only an undivided heart can experience true happiness.

Notes

1. For further study of the Hebrew understanding of the various parts of the body, see Hans Walter Wolff, *Anthropology of the Old Testament* (Philadelphia: Fortress Press, 1974).

2. Translations of the adjectives used to describe the heart vary. I have used the KJV words here.

3. Helmut Thielicke, *The Waiting Father: Sermons on the Parables of Jesus* (New York: Harper & Brothers, 1959), 151.

4. A. Cohen, *The Psalms.* Soncino Books of the Bible (London: The Soncino Press, 1945), 281.

5. Paul Tournier, *The Naming of Persons* (New York: Harper & Row, Publishers, 1975), 21.

5

Experiencing the Reality of Christ Through Obedience

Several years ago I led a Bible study in a church with several hundred attending. I stated that most of us do not experience as much of the reality of Christ's presence as we could. It was not a major emphasis of the study, but it triggered an unexpected response from a woman in the audience. Totally unself-conscious and with much emotion, she cried out, "But how can we know the presence of Christ?"

I stopped the study, and for the next few minutes attempted to answer her question as best I could "off the cuff." I realized afterwards that her anguished cry may express the longing of many sincere Christians who believe that the presence of Christ should be real but know that it isn't—at least not for them.

Whenever the disciples were with Jesus, we can sense the euphoria they experienced just from being with Him and listening to His words. Their fellowship with Him reached a climax in the upper room when He shared one last meal with them before His crucifixion. One of them, the one usually identified as John—the one Jesus loved, leaned against Jesus as they ate and talked (John 13:23). The sense of His powerful presence must have filled the room. We find ourselves envying their privilege to be in His presence and to know Him personally.

We know that Christians are supposed to be happy, so we try to look happy when on the inside we are as dry as the Sahara desert and want to cry when no one is looking.

We feel the guilt of our hypocrisy as we bravely sing, "When We Walk with the Lord," "I Stand Amazed in the Presence," "My Lord Is Near Me All the Time," "Just a Closer Walk with Thee," "In the Garden"—"He walks with me, and he talks with me," "Speak to my heart, Lord Jesus," and similar hymns. We hear other Christians claiming that Christ speaks to them, and we wonder why He doesn't speak to us. I heard one Christian leader confess recently that the inner voice which he tried to believe was the voice of Christ sounded like his own voice!

Were the promises of Christ empty mockeries? Did He really mean, "I am with you alway" (Matt. 28:20, KJV), "I will never fail you nor forsake you" (Heb. 13:5, RSV)? When Paul spoke about Christ being in him (Gal. 2:20), was he speaking idle words? If Christ is truly in us, then His presence should be real.

Let me make several clarifying statements before I continue. First, I believe that we can know the presence of Christ more authentically than we experience the presence of any human friend. I hasten to add that I am not into mystical experiences! I haven't had my first vision of Christ or heard His voice speaking audibly to me even once (and neither have most of the rest of us!) I also believe there are certain principles we can practice that will enable His presence to become more real to us. Let me share these ten principles with you. You will have to decide for yourself whether they are valid.

1. You Must Desire to Know Christ's Presence

What is the deepest desire of your heart? Would you be ashamed to share it with your closest friend? The deepest longing for the Christian ought to be to see our Lord, to sit at His feet, to embrace Him, to tell Him you love Him, and to hear Him tell you He loves you.

It is not necessary to experience death and resurrection in order to experience His reality (1 John 3:2). Unfortunately, most of us are content with much less of Christ's presence than He wants us to have. He stands at the door and knocks (Rev. 3:20) but does not force Himself on us.

I was listening intermittently on my car radio one day to a tape of a sermon that had been given to me when one statement arrested my attention. The preacher said, "We don't need more activity in the church; we don't need more prayer; we don't need more Bible study." I was thinking, *What kind of crackpot preacher is this?* Then I head the next statement: "No, we don't need these things. What we need is God." I realized the preacher was expressing the universal desire of all Christians to experience a greater sense of the reality of Christ. We

can be so involved in the forms of religion that we miss the reality of
our faith.

We must desire Christ's presence with the same kind of intense
longing found in the Psalms:

> As the deer pants for streams of water,
> so my soul pants for you, O God.
> My soul thirsts for God, for the living God.
> When can I go and meet with God? (Ps. 42:1-2).

> O God, you are my God,
> earnestly I seek you;
> my soul thirsts for you,
> my body longs for you,
>   in a dry and weary land
> where there is no water (Ps. 63:1).

> My heart and my flesh cry out
> for the living God (Ps. 84:2).

Intense desire is the first requirement if we are to experience God's
presence. When we desire Him with the same intensity as the psalm-
ists, we will not be disappointed.

2. Believe You Can Experience the Reality of Christ

Insisting that Christ is real is not a psychological aberration of a
sick mind. Nor is it positive thinking that says repeatedly "I think
He's real" until we convince ourselves that He is. Nor am I talking
about psychologically induced experiences such as hallucinations or
strange voices. I am speaking about the same kind of reality experienced by Moses, David, John, Paul, and many others through the
centuries.

We must believe that the promise of the Father and the Son are not
empty mockery. Our Lord said, "Never will I leave you;/ never will I
forsake you" (Heb. 13:5; see Deut. 31:6); "Surely I will be with you
always, to the very end of the age" (Matt. 28:20). James insisted,
"Come near to God and he will come near to you" (Jas. 4:8). Surely
these words have substance and should not be understood as shallow
theatrics of a disinterested God.

Most of us never tap the possibilities of what can be accomplished through faith. Does it make you as uncomfortable as it does me to read: "If you have faith as small as a mustard seed, you can say to this mountain, 'Move from here to there' and it will move" (Matt. 17:20)? I formerly tried to convince myself that Jesus was using typical oriental exaggeration to make a point that we could accomplish a great deal more than we do if our faith were stronger. But the unshakable conviction keeps disturbing me that Jesus meant exactly what He said. Literally, if we truly have even the smallest amount of faith, we can actually order a mountain to arise and float from one place to another! But which of us has moved our first anthill, let alone a mountain?

The greatest accomplishment of genuine faith would not be to move a mountain, however, but to experience the reality of Christ's presence. Like the father of the demon-possessed child, we want to cry out, "Help me overcome my unbelief!" even as we affirm, "I do believe" (Mark 9:24).

Believing that Christ can and wants to make Himself real to us is essential if the desire is to become reality.

3. Spend Time with Christ

Cultivating friendship on a human level requires the commitment of time to that other person. When a friendship has reached the once-a-year Christmas card stage, there is not much left of it. When someone telephones us or drops by to see us, we should be willing to stop whatever we are doing and give time to that relationship.

I have tried to analyze why time given to cultivating a friendship makes that relationship so meaningful. I finally realized that we are giving a part of our lives when we give time to another person, and that person is giving part of his or her life to us. This is true because life is made up of the hours and minutes allotted to us. We have no gift more valuable that we can give to a friend than our time because it represents part of our lives.

If a close friend comes to visit, you lay aside everything else and spend as much time as possible with that friend. You would adjust your schedule if necessary to be with the friend. You would not usher him or her to an upstairs room and say, "I hope to see you again sometime before you leave." I wonder, however, if we sometimes treat God that way in regard to the time we give Him.

If Christ is to be real, we must spend time with Him, even as time must be given to maintaining the closeness of a human relationship. But how do we spend time with Him?

We know the usual ways of spending time with our Lord: Bible study, prayer, and meditation. These are all good and necessary. However, they are so well known that there is no need to discuss them. There is, nevertheless, another way of spending time with Christ that most of us never discover. Few of us ever learn the secret of Nicholas Herman of Lorraine, France, better known as Brother Lawrence, which he revealed in the Christian classic: *The Practice of the Presence of God.* [1]

Brother Lawrence was admitted to a Carmelite monastic order in 1666 at the age of fifty-five after a life of soldiering and serving as a footman. He spent the remaining twenty-five years of his life practicing the presence of God while performing the most menial duties of cooking, washing dishes, working in the garden, or picking up straw. However, while performing these daily tasks, which most of us would brand as drudgery, he saw them as excellent opportunities for focusing on the presence of God. Instead of thinking about the dirty dishes he was washing, Brother Lawrence would commune with his Lord. He could call Christ the "Lord of the pots and pans."

All of us have those moments during the day which do not require any special concentration on what we are doing. Those are the times we can practice conversing with Him instead of letting our thoughts wander in other paths. We can talk to Him while driving to work or while waiting for a bus. Waiting in an outer office for an appointment, jogging early in the morning, sitting in church waiting for the service to begin, even washing dishes are all excellent opportunities for developing the practice of the presence of God. We can tell Him all our problems, doubts, fears, anxieties, anger, and frustrations. Whatever concerns us concerns Him. At the same time, however, we should not forgot to tell Him of our love for Him.

Lovers like to tell each other how much they love the other. They never get tired of thinking of new ways to verbalize their love. Parents also enjoy hearing a child express love. Suppose your child comes to you and says, "I don't want anything—no new toy, no increase in allowance. I just want to tell you I love you." We know how much that unsolicited expression of love would mean to us. I believe it would mean as much to God for us to tell Him we love Him. If we analyze the content of our prayers, we will probably discover that at least 80 percent of them are prayers asking for something or complaining. God is not unwilling to hear our requests or our problems, but He would like to hear our expressions of love, also.

I heard about the mother who told her little girl to go upstairs and prepare for bed. "Say your prayers, and I will come up later to tuck you in." In a few minutes the mother came to the child's bedside and asked, "Did you say your prayers tonight?" The child responded, "No, I didn't. I think God must get tired of hearing the same old prayer night after night, so I pulled the covers over my head and told him the story of the three bears!" I am quite sure that prayer delighted God much more than "Now I lay me down to sleep."

Prayer to God is not getting all our "Thees" and Thous" straight, nor is it sounding just the right note of solemnity and piety in our words. True prayer is conversing with God as you would with a best friend. You share everything, holding back nothing. Fenelon, a seventeenth-century archbishop at the court of Louis XIV, wisely advised his friends, "When you pray, let your prayers be simple loving prayers out of the heart. This is far better than more refined prayers which come only from the head."[2]

Here is the principle: we experience the reality of Christ's presence in direct proportion to the time we spend with Him.

4. Do Not Allow Sins to Remain Unconfessed

Unconfessed sin is like a wall built between you and God. Each sin not dealt with immediately adds another brick, row by row, until the wall shuts out the presence of God. We are warned,

> Your iniquities have separated
> you from your God;
> your sins have hidden his face from you,
> so that he will not hear (Isa. 59:2).

God is a God who both reveals and hides Himself. We are more familiar with the God who reveals, whether in nature (Ps. 19:1), events (the Exodus, the Cross), people (the prophets), His word (Heb.

4:12), and, of course, supremely in Christ (John 14:9). God also is the God who hides Himself. We are familiar with hiding from God. The human race has been doing that ever since the first man and woman hid from God in the garden of Eden (Gen. 3:10). We are not so familiar with the biblical emphasis that God sometimes hides from us (see Job 13:24; Ps. 44:24; Isa. 1:15; 45:15)!

Why would God hide Himself from us? We must emphatically insist that His hiddenness is not the result of disinterest. The cross is our constant reminder of His intense interest in us. The most obvious reason for God's hiding is to show disapproval of what we are doing (Isa. 59:2; Mic. 3:4). If God seems far away, if you are cold toward Him, and if your prayers seem to bounce back in your face as though heaven were made of iron, there is probably a sin that has not been confessed.

It may be the sin of a wrong ambition. All ambition is not wrong, but if achieving our desired goals separates us from the presence of God, it is not worth the cost. Moses understood that reaching the Promised Land, as desirable a goal as it was, was not worth sacrificing the ongoing presence of God. When the Israelites worshiped the golden calf, God was so angry that He was at first determined to destroy them. Through Moses' intercession, God relented and agreed to keep His word to bring the people to the Promised Land, but God said His presence would not go with them because He could become angry enough again to destroy them.

Moses continued to plead, and God agreed that His presence would be with them from time to time (Ex. 33:14; the verb "will go" suggests occasional but not continual action). That was not sufficient for Moses. He appealed once more, "If your Presence does not go with us, do not send us up from here" (Ex. 33:15; the participle "go" expresses continuous, unbroken action; here it could be translated, "go with us all the time"). Moses insisted that the one thing that makes God's people distinct from all other peoples on the face of the earth is the presence of God (Ex. 33:16). Moses understood that no success we may achieve is worth the cost if it means sacrificing the abiding presence of God.

If sin is separating us from the Lord's presence, there is a way to remove the barrier. "If we confess our sins, he is faithful and just and will forgive us our sins and purify us from all unrighteousness" (1

John 1:9). When we confess our sins, the walls that separate us from God will come tumbling down.

5. Be Willing to Obey God's Commands

Obedience is the best evidence of trust in God. We make excuses for not living a consistent Christian life, for not answering God's call, for not going to the mission field, or for not giving up something that seems important to us. However, the real root of our problem is that we do not really have confidence that God's ways and plans for us are better than ours (see Jer. 29:11; Rom. 12:2).

Disobedience is sin, and sin drives a wedge between us and God just as Adam and Eve hid from God when they were disobedient. Dietrich Bonhoeffer, a martyr for the faith in Nazi Germany during World War II, insisted that obedience is a test of true faith. He said, "Only he who believes is obedient, and only he who is obedient believes."[3] Bonhoeffer further asserted that "the step of obedience must be taken before faith can be possible. Unless he obeys, a man cannot believe"[4] (See John 6:29.)

Not only is obedience vital for faith, but it is also necessary for maintaining an unbroken sense of the presence of Christ.

Often overlooked, a brief statement in John 14:21 has much to say about experiencing the presence of Christ. Jesus said, "Whoever has my commands and obeys them, . . . I too will love him and show myself to him." The *King James Version* says, "I . . . will manifest myself to him." The Williams translation brought it out clearly to me for the first time: "Whoever continues to hold and keep my commands, . . . I will love him myself and will make myself real to him."[5]

There could be no plainer statement than this one. It is a promise by Christ Himself that He will make Himself real to those who obey His commands. Obedience is the single most important key for experiencing the reality of the presence of Christ.

6. Admit Your Total Dependence on Christ

John 15:5 says, "Apart from me you can do nothing." We can easily repeat these words, but do we really believe them? Of course not! We do many things without Him. We make our own plans and carry them out without ever seeking His approval. Sometimes as an afterthought we offer a quick prayer: "Lord, bless what I have already decided to do!" No wonder so many of our carefully made plans never accomplish what we hoped they would.

One of childhood's unforgettable memories is that of flying a kite. I can still remember the tense moments when the kite swayed drunkenly back and forth before the wind caught it solidly and began to lift it into the air. Sometimes the kite would soar so high in the sky that it was lost to sight. Only the tug on the string in my hand gave assurance that it was still at the other end of the string.

Suppose, however, that the soaring kite could speak and say, "Now cut me loose. I'm soaring. I don't need you any longer." We know what would happen. The kite would quickly come crashing to the ground. But isn't that often our attitude? When things are going well, and we seem to be accomplishing our plans, our attitude is the same as the kite's: "Lord, cut me loose; I don't need You any longer." The results will be equally as disastrous as those of the kite.

Though we may not express our attitude in words, our neglect often says, "Lord, I don't need You anymore." Is it any wonder that we do not experience the presence of Christ?

7. Simplify Your Life-style

Most of us live our lives at too hectic a pace. We clutter our days with too many activities. We want too much. We could not hear the still small voice even if it were amplified to the roar of an erupting volcano.

The simplicity of Jesus' life-style ought to be our model. He did not have a place He could call His own to go to bed at night (Matt. 8:20). When He died, the only article of clothing He possessed was the garment for which the Roman soldiers cast lots (Matt. 27:35). I do not mean to suggest that the Scriptures tell us to get rid of all our possessions or that material possessions in themselves are evil. However, when things begin to possess and control us and take priority over everything else, they become a hindrance to experiencing the reality of Christ. I have been in many homes that are cluttered with so many "things" that it is often necessary to tread a narrow path between them to go from room to room!

Most of us could look around our homes and find many things we really do not need. These possessions could be sold and the money sent to feed or clothe a desperately needy child in another part of the world. When I went to Brazil as a missionary, I had the same problem with possessions as most people. However, when I saw the acute poverty there, something in me changed. On two occasions I saw people fall dead on busy city streets from hunger or disease. I saw small children digging in garbage cans to find a scrap of food. Since those experiences I have never been able to hold on as tightly to "things" as I did before.

Fenelon gave good advice. He said, "We can learn a lesson from babies. Babies own nothing. They treat diamonds and apples alike. Be like babies. Have nothing of your own. It all belongs to God, anyway."[6]

Possessions can be a hindrance to fellowship with Christ. One day a rich young ruler came to Jesus. He seemed to be sincere in his search for eternal life. After questioning him in regard to morality, Jesus called attention to the one thing standing between him and being a disciple of Jesus— his wealth. Jesus challenged the youth to give up his wealth and to follow Him. Faced with the choice, the young man found it impossible to let go of his possessions and went away very sad (Matt. 19:16-22; Luke 18:18-25). Those possessions had separated him from Christ. Our possessions will not cause us to lose our salvation, but they can separate us from the reality of the vital presence of Christ.

Do we have biblical support for simplifying our life-styles? Yes, we do. Paul reminded us that Satan is the one who deceives us and leads us away from simplicity (2 Cor. 11:3). We find ourselves grasping for more possessions like everyone else. Paul reminded us that this is conforming to the world (Rom. 12:2). John warned us not to love the world or the things in the world (1 John 2:15).

If you have never read Richard Foster's *Freedom of Simplicity*,[7] I recommend it. You will never again have the same attitude toward possessions as you once did after reading this book.

8. Be Careful What You Think About

If we saturate our minds with pornographic thoughts and our vision with x-rated films, they will be like snow on the TV set, static on the radio, or dirt on a window. They effectively shut out a clear view of Christ, and He becomes blurred and indistinct.

Pornography has become a national tragedy. Like the anesthetic that dulls the pain of surgery, pornography dulls our moral sensitivity so that we find it increasingly difficult to distinguish moral from immoral behavior (see Isa. 5:20 for a picture of moral confusion centuries ago). As evidence of pornography's insidious nature, most of us calmly view scenes on television today in our homes that would have shocked us twenty years ago. It might surprise us to discover how many regular churchgoers read pornographic magazines and view x-rated films in the privacy of their homes. The time they spend absorbed in pornographic materials often exceeds the time they spend in Bible reading.

Some who have been delivered from the bondage of pornography say it is like a habit-forming drug. Like drugs, it requires a stronger and stronger, cruder and cruder, kind of pornography to maintain the same level of stimulation. Once a person is "hooked" on pornography, it is not easily given up.

Philippians 4:8 would not be popular advice for most people today, but it is still valid advice for Christians: "Whatever is true, whatever is noble, whatever is right, whatever is pure, whatever is lovely, whatever is admirable—if anything is excellent or praiseworthy—think about such things."

It is impossible to experience the reality of the presence of Christ when our minds are saturated with pornographic images. You cannot have both. You have to decide which you prefer.

9. Love Other Christians

One of the most appealing characteristics of early Christians was their love for one another. Their love drew others irresistibly to Christ like a magnet draws metal. Unfortunately, the world looks at us today and is not convinced by what it sees that we love one another. What it often sees are critical attitudes, hurt feelings, church members not speaking to each other, pastors driven out of their churches by angry congregations, and church and denominational splits. Sometimes lost people are more civil to one another than Christians are to other Christians!

There is a unique awareness of the presence of Christ when we love other Christians. This can be experienced by one individual or by an entire church. Simone Weil, a twentieth-century mystic, in her book *Waiting for God* wrote with unusual perception: "Nothing among human things has such power to keep our gaze fixed ever more intensely upon God, than friendship for the friends of God."[8]

Earlier in this chapter I listed the willingness to obey God's commands as a key element for experiencing the reality of Christ's presence. I based the statement on John 14:21, but I want to return to that verse for another emphasis.

When I first read Williams's translation, "Whoever continues to hold and keep my commands, . . . I will love him myself and will make myself real to him," I was impressed by the importance of obeying God's commands to experience the reality of Christ. However, the verse raised another question in my mind. Was Jesus saying that we must return to the legalistic bondage of the Old Testament laws—do this, don't do that—in order for His presence to be real to us? That kind of reasoning seemed to be flawed. Had not Jesus reinterpreted the law Himself? In fact, He summed up the spirit of the law in one statement: "In everything, do to others what you would have them do to you, for this sums up the Law and the Prophets" (Matt. 7:12). The apostle Paul also strongly warned that we not be deceived to return to the bondage of legalism (Gal. 3:1-3,10-14).

As I struggled to understand John 14:21, I was confused. I saw that it contained the clearest statement for knowing how to experience the reality of Christ to be found in the New Testament. Yet it seemed to require that we abandon grace and return to Old Testament legalism. I found myself asking, "Lord, which commands do You mean that I should obey?" Then I realized as I continued reading through the rest of chapter 14 and into chapter 15 that I had been hearing the answer to my question since beginning my reading in chapter 13. Which commands? Listen to John 13:34: "A new commandment I give you: Love one another." Add to that: "My command is this: Love each other as I have loved you" (John 15:12), and "This is my command: Love each other" (John 15:17). The same emphasis is repeated in 1 John 2:7-11; 3:11; 3:23; 4:7-12; 4:21. No command is emphasized more frequently in the New Testament than the command to love one another.

Therefore, I believe that we are justified in interpreting John 14:21 to mean that by obeying the command to love one another, Christ will make Himself real to us. I encourage you to establish a meaningful, open relationship with one or two Christians, if you have never done this. It will require courage to be open, vulnerable, transparent, caring, patient, self-sacrificing, and authentic; but it will be worth it. You will discover a new dimension to Christ's reality through those relationships.

I have tried to understand why loving one another is such a vital element in experiencing the reality of Christ. I concluded that though we agree that God is Spirit and that we must worship Him in spirit and in truth (John 4:24), we live in the realm of the five senses. For us reality must be perceived through these five senses. We can love Christ more easily when we see Him enfleshed in the life of another Christian. Like doubting Thomas (John 20:25), we have to see and to touch in order to believe.

How many times have you heard people describing their conversion with words like these: "I saw something in that person's life I did not have, and I wanted it." Though they did not understand fully, they were seeing Christ through that person in a way they never would have seen Him by reading a thousand learned theological books.

When Moses came down from Mount Sinai, his face glistened so brightly from being in the presence of God that the people were afraid to come near him (Ex. 34:29-30). It is unlikely that people will have to put on sunglasses for protection against the glow when they look at you and me! However, there ought to be an intangible, indefinable quality about the Christian that sets us apart. Moses said the quality that distinguishes us from all other peoples on the face of the earth is the presence of God (Ex. 33:16).

10. Express Your Love Verbally to Christ

When was the last time you told your spouse or your children that you loved them? Or a close friend? If you can't remember, it has been too long. I heard about one man who said he told his wife thirty-five years ago on their wedding day that he loved her, and once was enough! He didn't want to spoil her!

I once read about a husband and wife who during the forty-nine years of their marriage had a custom of saying to each other before going to sleep: "Good night, Sweetheart. I love you." The other would reply, "Thank you. Good night, Sweetheart. I love you." I calculated that during those forty-nine years the words *I love you* were repeated 35,770 times. I am sure they never got tired of saying and hearing those three little words.

Lovers never tire of telling each other how much they love the other because of the delight it brings to both of them. Only when the glow of love has faded do we fail to experience happiness in telling each other of our love.

It can be a frustrating experience to see a beautiful sunset and be unable to tell someone about it. It probably would be frustrating to a pastor to make a hole in one on Sunday afternoon because he cannot tell anyone about it! It would be frustrating if we could never tell God that we love Him, but we can whenever we desire. There is a popular bumper sticker that says, "Have you hugged your kids today?" Perhaps it should be modified to read, "Have you told God today that you love Him?"

How do we tell God that we love Him? Answer: the same way we would tell our spouse or friend! Try for a few days to tell God you love Him the first thing when you awake in the morning. You will be surprised at the difference it will make in the day.

Conclusion

Our Lord did not create us primarily to be busy, to study the Bible, to pray, to preach, or even to witness. He created us first of all to have fellowship with Him. The Presbyterian Shorter Catechism asks the question: "What is the chief end of man?" The answer to be given is: "Man's chief end is to glorify God and to enjoy him forever." It is true that we will enjoy fellowship with God in eternity, but we ought to enjoy it now. As the reality of Christ's presence becomes more authentic in our experience, we discover an outward calm, inner peace, resources for any situation, the happiness that comes with being in love, and a life that will draw others to Christ.

From whatever angle we examine the Christian life, we keep returning to obedience as the key to happiness. Obedience enables us to have an undivided heart. It also enables us to experience the reality of

Christ's presence.

Principle: Obedience in all areas of life is the key to experiencing the reality of Christ's presence.

Notes

1. Brother Lawrence, *The Practice of the Presence of God* (New York: Fleming H. Revell Co., 1895).

2. Fenelon, *Let Go* (Springdale, Pa.: Whitaker House, 1973), 30.

3. Dietrich Bonhoeffer, *The Cost of Discipleship* (first published 1949; reprint, New York: The Macmillan Co., 1963), 69.

4. Ibid., 72.

5. Charles B. Williams, *The New Testament: A Private Translation in the Language of the People* (Bruce Humphries, Inc., 1937; reprint, Chicago: Moody Press, 1957).

6. Fenelon, *Let Go*, 30.

7. Richard Foster, *Freedom of Simplicity* (San Francisco: Harper & Row, Publishers, 1981).

8. Simone Weil, *Waiting for God* (G. P. Putnam's Sons, 1951; reprint, New York/San Francisco: Harper & Row, Publishers, 1973), 74.

6
Happiness Is Making Right Choices

All of us are constantly confronted with making choices every day from the moment we wake up. We choose whether to get up immediately or roll over for another ten minutes' sleep! We must choose what we will wear that day. We choose what kind of breakfast to eat. Throughout the day decisions of all kinds must be made. Many of them require little thought because the choices have become part of our daily routine. The route we drive to work, the office we work in, the chair we occupy at mealtime, or the toothbrush we use have become so habitual that we do not consciously think about them.

Good or Better?

Sometimes we are confronted with several choices, none of which would be particularly wrong. However, there are those rare moments when making the right choice can be extremely important, even life changing. Those are the times when we find ourselves agonizing about what to do. In those situations a mistake could be disastrous, whereas the right choice will bring desirable consequences. Those are the times when we ask, "How can I know how to make the right choice?" This chapter will attempt to address that question.

If you had been in the little village of Bethany a few miles east of Jerusalem about 2,000 years ago, you might have noticed a man hurrying away from his house one morning. If you had asked a neighbor about his identify, he would have replied, "That's Lazarus. He lives in that house with his two sisters, Mary and Martha." Your curiosity about Lazarus's obvious haste might cause you to catch up with him to ask why he was leaving in such haste. He would have replied, "Company is coming, and I learned long ago that I can be of most help by getting out of the way while my sisters are cleaning and cooking."

On further inquiry you would learn that the expected guest was their friend Jesus, who made it a point to visit them whenever He was in Bethany.

Occasionally, while visiting for the church and walking up the sidewalk toward a house, I have heard a voice from within shout loudly, "The preacher is coming!" Standing at the door, I could hear the sound of running feet and doors slamming. I have never been sure what was taking place in those moments. Perhaps a few family skeletons were being hastily shoved into a closet! I have suspected that a frantic search was under way to find a Bible, dust it off, and place it on prominent view in the living room before opening the door!

Even when unexpected company comes, we like for everything to be just right to make a favorable impression on our guest. When we know in advance of an impending visit, the activity can be extremely hectic if the host is a perfectionist. Martha was one of those. She wanted everything to be just right when Jesus arrived. She was the kind who would make sure every picture on the wall is straight, every chair is at just the right angle in the room, and, of course, there would be no dust anywhere!

My own mother was that kind of person when preparing for company. Even though she knew her guests would go no further than the front room, she made sure that even the furniture in the upstairs back bedroom was dusted. I occasionally tried to tell her that such meticulous effort was unnecessary. I never understood her logic, and she always ignored mine when preparing for company.

When Jesus arrived, Martha was probably flushed and flustered from all her exertion. She greeted Him hurriedly and rushed back to the kitchen to tell her sister Mary that the company had arrived. But Mary was not to be found anywhere. The thought must then have crossed Martha's mind, *Surely my sister wouldn't remain in the room with the men.* But when Martha entered the room, she saw Mary sitting quietly in the shadows in a corner absorbed in every word of Jesus. Mary was oblivious of her neglected household duties and the breach of custom that normally separated men from women (see John 4:27).

Seeing her was too much for Martha. She interrupted Jesus' words and began to unbraid Him! He may have been discussing His coming death or explaining a statement He had made in the Sermon on the Mount, but that did not matter to Martha. She scolded Him, "Lord, don't you care that my sister has left me to do the work by myself? Tell her to help me!" (Luke 10:40).

How much Martha is like us! We hurt the ones we love the most with our sharp words and inconsiderate actions. We are often more courteous with strangers or casual acquaintances than with those closest to us. If you want to know what a person is really like, don't ask friends or acquaintances. Ask the members of the family, for they know us best.

Jesus must have looked from Martha to Mary and grasped the situation in a moment. Martha thought the way to please Him was by providing a neat house and good food. Mary only wanted to listen to His words.

Our Lord frequently judges matters differently from the way we do. He often does not consider the things which seem important to us. He gently chided Martha: "Martha, Martha, you are worried and bothered about so many things; but only a few things are necessary, really only one, for Mary has chosen the good part, which shall not be taken away from her" (Luke 10:41-42, NASB).

In His teachings Jesus always used language with which His hearers could identify. He never tried to impress them with His vocabulary, for it was more important they understand Him. Whether with shepherd, scribe, priest, or soldier, He could use figures of speech they could understand. Today if Jesus were with a doctor, an engineer, or a farmer, He would use language each of them could understand.

Jesus was using a word Martha would have understood when He said Mary had chosen the "good part." It is a word that could describe a choice cut of meat purchased at the market by one with a sharp eye. It could describe a plump cluster of grapes with just the right color and flavor or the red, sweet center of a melon. For me the choice bit— the "good part"—is the center of a cinnamon roll. It always seems to have just a little more cinnamon and frosting than the rest so I carefully save it for the last bite. Some people eat cinnamon rolls by starting at one side and going straight through to the other, like Sherman's march through Georgia! I like to start at the outside of the spiral and work my way slowly around to that last choice bite in the center.

Martha and Mary both loved Jesus. Each one made a choice as to how she would express that love. Martha showed her love by her activity. Mary showed hers by her desire to sit at the feet of Jesus and hear His words. Martha's choice was not evil. Her intentions were good, but she did not make the best choice. She needed to heed the advice of a plaque that one pastor kept on his desk: "Come apart before you come apart."

Life's choices are not always between good and evil, but between good and better. Few of us deliberately make a wrong choice that we know will hurt or destroy us. Even when it is a wrong choice, we rationalize that it is not.

The choice between that which is clearly good and evil is not difficult to make. However, sometimes the right choice is not so easy to make as it falls in a "gray" area. It may or may not appear to be the best choice. Jeremiah confronted the people of Judah in his day with making a choice that seemed preposterous. He warned them that if they did not submit to Babylonia, their own nation would be destroyed (21:8-10). The people refused to believe him. Jeremiah's advice to surrender to the enemy seemed treasonous, but it would have saved them from destruction.

Making Right Choices

Israel had a history of making wrong choices. The people chose to worship Baal and give him credit for their blessings rather than God (Hos. 2:8). They chose to place their confidence in the political and military might of other nations rather than in God (2 Kings 16:7; Hos. 7:11). They believed their false prophets rather than the true prophets (Mic. 2:11; Jer. 7:4). They chose to depend on their own abilities rather than on God (Hos. 12:8). Only when Jerusalem and its temple lay in smoldering ruins did some of the people realize they had made wrong choices.

From our perspective we say they should have known better. They should have known that Jeremiah was God's true prophet, and they should have listened to his warnings and the warnings of prophets like him. Judah's tragedy serves as a reminder that right choices are not always easy to make. People do not deliberately make choices that they believe will harm or destroy them.

The question constantly confronts all of us: How can I know how to make right choices? This is not a new question. The first man and woman were confronted with a choice in Eden. It was to obey God or disobey and eat the forbidden fruit. If they had obeyed, they would have found an unending happiness in the garden of Eden. They chose to disobey and were driven from the garden.

When Moses told the people at Mount Sinai that God was willing to make a covenant with them if they would obey His laws, without hesitation they replied, "Everything the Lord has said we will do" (Ex. 24:3). Unfortunately, their subsequent actions did not match their words. There was never an extended period in Israel's history when the people obeyed God. Consequently, they forfeited the covenant blessings He had promised them.

Just before coming to the end of his years as Israel's leader, Joshua confronted the people with a choice: "Choose for yourselves this day whom you will serve, whether the gods your forefathers served beyond the River, or the gods of the Amorites, in whose land you are living. But as for me and my household, we will serve the Lord" (24:15). Their response was: "We will serve the Lord" (24:21). Once again, Israel's subsequent history showed their insincerity.

Abraham chose to believe God, and it was credited to him as righteousness (Rom. 4:3). Moses "chose to be mistreated along with the people of God rather than to enjoy the pleasures of sin for a short time" (Heb. 11:25). Samuel chose to continue praying for Israel even though the people rejected him as their leader (1 Sam. 12:23). David chose not to kill God's anointed ruler, Saul, when he had the opportunities (1 Sam. 24:1-22; 26:1-25). Solomon chose a discerning heart (Hebrew, "listening heart") instead of great wealth and fame (1 Kings 3:5-14).

Elijah chose to follow God rather than Baal (1 Kings 18). Isaiah chose to accept God's call to be His prophet (Isa. 6:8). Hezekiah chose to trust in God. The Scriptures say there was no one like him among the kings of Judah before or after him (2 Kings 18:5). Esther chose to risk the loss of her life in order to save her people from destruction (Esther 4:16). Nehemiah chose to return to Jerusalem to help the people rebuild the city walls rather than continue a life of privilege in the Persian court (Neh. 2:4-5). Paul chose to give up everything in order to be identified with Christ (Phil. 3:8).

In every case, those men and women in the Bible made the right choices by deciding to obey God rather than their own desires, human logic, or the wishes of others. Those who chose to obey God received His approval. Even when their choices resulted in hardship, and sometimes in death, none of them ever concluded that it was a mistake to obey God.

It is difficult to make our own decisions, but sometimes we are asked to help someone else make a decision. Rare are those individuals who have never been asked, "What should I do in this situation?" Sometimes the answer is easy, especially if it involves a clear matter of right or wrong. However, all decisions are not so clear-cut.

In my capacity as a seminary teacher, students come to me from time to time asking, "What should I do?" One student had an invitation to try out for a professional football team, a dream from high school days. He asked me if he should accept it or continue his studies for the ministry. Frequently students ask me if they should pursue graduate studies beyond their basic theological degree. Two weeks ago a former student telephoned me from another state to ask for help in deciding whether he had been called by God to be a foreign missionary. A single pastor called me to ask if he should marry a widow with two small children. Another pastor called to ask if he should perform the marriage of a couple whose parents were opposed to the marriage.

If sometimes it is difficult to make decisions that only involve ourselves, how much more difficult when someone asks us for help when they are confronted with choices.

Principles for Right Decision Making

There are some principles that can be followed when we are sincerely trying to make the right decision, that is, one that will please God as well as being in our best interest.

First, the right choice will never conflict with the moral principles found in the Scriptures. Occasionally, a newspaper story quotes a murderer: "God told me to do it." The murderer may have heard a voice saying "do it," but it was not God's voice! Murder is a violation of God's moral laws (Ex. 20:13). He will not ask us to violate moral principles that He has established.

Second, the right choice will bring a feeling of assurance and inner peace. Sometimes we cannot know whether the choice was the right one until after we make it. Moses' confirmation that God had sent him to deliver Israel from slavery in Egypt came when, after delivering them, Moses returned with the people to Mount Sinai to worship God (Ex. 3:10-12; 19:1).

I resisted for almost six years what I knew was God's certain call for me to enter the ministry. During that time I found all kinds of convincing reasons why I should not be a preacher, but I never was at peace with myself during those years, and they were largely unproductive years. Only when I finally said: "Lord, I am willing to do whatever You want me to do with my life" did that elusive peace and inner tranquillity became a reality. Obedience truly is the gateway to happiness!

A third principle for making right choices is to have an attitude of willingness to obey God in whatever He would have us do. When confronted with a choice of accepting the cross or drawing back from it, our Lord struggled in the garden of Gethsemane until He could say, "Not as I will, but as you will" (Matt. 26:39). Once that decision was made to obey God, Jesus never looked back.

Two friends of mine from high school days were confronted with a choice in an unusual way. Shortly after my own conversion experience at age twenty-four, I told them what had happened to me. Their first reaction was that I had lost my mind! However, within a few weeks they also found themselves torn between a decision to accept or reject Christ. At that time they had recently been blessed with the birth of a baby girl after having been told by physicians for the first five years of their marriage that they could not have children.

They called me one evening to say that they were going to accept Christ that night or else put Him out of their lives forever. Later that evening they called again to tell me what had happened. The couple went into separate rooms in order not to influence the other's decision. As the husband prayed, he sensed that God was asking, "Would you be willing to give up this baby you love so much in order to have Christ?" The question angered him, and he bitterly fought against it, but finally made the choice that he must have Christ as his Lord at any cost.

He jumped up and ran to tell his wife about his decision. They almost collided in the hall, as at the same moment she was coming to tell him an experience that proved to be identical with his! They both made the right choice, but God did not take away their child. It has never been His intention to do so, but they had to discover, as many others have, that Christ becomes our Lord and Savior only when we are willing to give up everything for Him (Jer. 29:13; Matt. 10:37-39; 13:44-45). Not only did the Lord *not* take their baby from my friends; He later gave them two more children!

Summary

This entire book is a study on how to experience happiness. In the second chapter obedience to God was seen as the "key" or gateway to happiness. It was followed by a chapter suggesting applications of the principle. Then the next chapter explored one of the major causes of unhappiness—a life fragmented by indecision and uncertainty. It concluded that the serene, happy person has an undivided heart which is the result of a commitment to obey God. The fifth chapter examined the longing which all of us have for a more authentic experience with the reality of Christ. Obedience was shown to be the key to knowing that reality, especially obedience with regard to the command to love others (John 14:21; 15:12,17).

The purpose of this chapter has been to show that a major source of unhappiness is the inability to make decisions, especially right ones, and that wrong choices will bring profound unhappiness. We are less likely to make the wrong choices if we have made a prior commitment to obey Christ in whatever choices we make. Perhaps the message is beginning to sound like a broken record, but from whatever angle we approach life, obedience to God is clearly evident as the key for finding happiness.

Principle: Obedience to God enables us to make right choices, and right choices bring happiness.

7

God's Plan and Your Happiness

A wise rabbi once observed that we experience seven stages during our lifetimes. At one year of age we are like a king, with everyone embracing us and honoring our every desire. At age two and three we are like a pig wallowing in the mud, poking about and putting every loose object found in our mouths. At ten we skip about with the vigor of a young goat. At twenty we whinny like a horse and seek a mate. After marriage we bear the burdens and responsibilities of life like a donkey. In the mid-years we harden our faces like a dog in search of food for survival. Finally, in old age we are stooped and grunting like an ape![1] Not a very pretty picture of life, but life for many is no more than a dreary hopeless cycle of birth to death because they never discover any purpose for their existence.

The adolescent years are surely the most wonderful and at the same time the most frightening time of life. The teenager looks in the mirror and sees the metamorphosis from child to adult taking place before his or her eyes. Thoughts and urges fill their minds that had never been there before. A desire for independence from parental control develops, more violently for some than for others. Above all else, a nagging question that was never considered during the carefree days of childhood cannot be ignored: What am I going to do with my life?

The most thrilling statement in the Bible that we may ever read are the words of the prophet Jeremiah: " 'For I know the plans I have for you,' declares the Lord, 'plans to prosper you and not to harm you, plans to give you a hope and a future' " (29:11). Jeremiah spoke these words to the people of Judah at a time when their future appeared bleak and hopeless. The mighty Babylonians were rapidly bringing all the surrounding nations of the ancient Near East under their control.

It appeared that little Judah was marked for destruction, but in the midst of what appeared to be a hopeless situation, God assured the people that there was a future for them in His plans.

God Has a Plan for Each of Us

I do not believe that we do violence to Jeremiah's words addressed to Judah by personalizing them to say that God has a plan for each of us. Applied to each of us individually, the verse has some important implications.

First, it suggests that the God who created the entire universe and all that is in it knows each of us personally. Jesus said that no sparrow falls to the ground without God's knowledge and that even the hairs of our head are numbered (Matt. 10:29-30). In an era of exploding populations when we are often treated as numbers rather than persons, it is easy to wonder if anyone cares whether we live or die. In such an impersonal world it is reassuring to know that God knows us personally. If God is on our side, it does not really matter if the whole world is indifferent to us (Rom. 8:31).

However, the verse implies more than God's knowledge of our existence. It also suggests that He cares for us. He cares for us enough to make plans for us, plans that will bring fulfillment and happiness. If He cares for us, it must also mean that we are important to Him. How important? We are so important that He gave His only Son so that we could have eternal life (John 3:16).

God Has Always Had a Plan for Us

If the fact that God has a plan for each of us is not enough to blow our minds, we are reminded elsewhere in the Scriptures that God has always had a plan for us, even before the creation of the world! Read carefully Psalm 139:4,16; Isaiah 49:1; Jeremiah 1:5; Galatians 1:15; and Ephesians 1:4. We may never fully understand all that these verses are saying, but they do affirm that God's plan for us is not a hasty afterthought or an idle pastime to occupy His endless afternoons! Instead, it is the result of deliberate planning even before we ever existed!

God's Plan Is Better Than Any We Could Devise

If God has devised a plan that will bring fulfillment and not harm to us, it is better than any plan we could ever concoct.

Some would object by saying that God has given us sufficient intelligence to take inventory of ourselves and determine what is best for us. They argue that for God to impose a plan on us would take away our freedom and happiness. The best reply to that kind of argument is to look about at the unhappy millions who are following their own ways but never find genuine contentment or a sense of purpose. By contrast, I have never met a person who has obediently followed God's plan who said, "If I could live life over again, I would to it differently."

I heard a recently retired missionary of forty years service reflect on her career before an audience of 5,000 young people. The interviewer asked, "If you could live those forty years over, would you do it differently?" Without hesitation she replied, "I wouldn't change a thing!" She had learned long before that God's plan for her life was better than any she could have devised.

John Wesley was once asked, "If you knew you were going to die at midnight tomorrow, how would you spend the few remaining hours allotted to you?" He replied that he would spend the remaining hours just as he had already planned, preaching that evening and again at 5:00 the next morning and twice more that day. In the evening I would retire to my room, he said, "commend myself to my heavenly Father, lie down to rest, and wake up in Glory."

Why is God's plan better than any we could devise? The answer is found in the fact that we are happiest doing what we do best. As Christians we believe that we are born with certain God-given gifts or talents (Rom. 12:4-8; 1 Cor. 12:4-11). Since God gives us these gifts, He knows what we are best suited to do. As we discover our gifts, develop, and use them, we find that we experience the greatest joy and satisfaction doing the things that make use of those gifts.

The person who is not gifted with musical ability would be miserable trying to have a career as a singer. A color-blind person would be terribly frustrated trying to be an artist. A person without mathematical ability would never have a successful career as an engineer. Many people view their work as a necessary burden that must be endured in order to provide for the needs of their family. They can hardly wait until the weekend to escape their job. Their motto is TGIF: "Thank goodness, it's Friday!" They cannot understand persons who say they enjoy their work.

The story has been told of a man at the side of the road frantically tinkering with his Model-T Ford to get it started, but without success. A chauffeur-driven car stopped, and an expensively dressed man got out. After watching the futile efforts of the man to start his car, the stranger suggested a minor adjustment that he should make in the engine. The owner was skeptical but was willing to try anything. He made the adjustment, and when he cranked the car, the motor began to run like new. Amazed, the man asked the stranger how he knew what to do. The answer was, "I'm Henry Ford. I made the car, so I know all about how it works."[2] Since God made us and gave us our talents and aptitudes, He also knows what we are best equipped to do.

If we are happiest doing what we do best, and God is the One who knows what we are best suited to do, why are so many unwilling to accept God's plan for their lives? Numerous answers could be given to that question, but I believe His plan is most often rejected because of a belief that it is some kind of bitter pill to swallow. Many people reject God's plan because they believe they would have to give up all of life's pleasures or because their own ambitions are more appealing.

Like many others, I violently resisted God's clear call for me to become a foreign missionary. I did not want to give up the plans I had made. Leaving home, friends, and family to live in a strange culture did not appeal to me as being the most happy, fulfilling life. One day, however, I read Romans 12:2: "Do not conform any longer to the pattern of this world, but be transformed by the renewing of your mind. Then you will be able to test and approve what God's will is— his good, pleasing and perfect will."

I had read the verse many times, but on that day I understood it for the first time. What could be better than living a life that is good, pleasing, and perfect? From that moment I could no longer say no to God's plan for my life.

God Wants Us to Know His Plan for Us

You may be thinking, *That is all well and good, but how can I know what that plan is? Do I stumble along and hope that somewhere down the way I will find myself carrying out God's plan for me?* One of the psalms says: "I will instruct you and teach you in the way you should go" (Ps. 32:8). A proverb states:

> Trust in the Lord with all your heart
> and lean not on your own understanding;
> in all your ways acknowledge him,
> and he will make your paths straight
> (Prov. 3:5-6; "He shall direct thy paths," KJV).

Paul wrote, "Do not be foolish, but understand what the Lord's will is" (Eph. 5:17). Since God has made a plan for our lives, it is reasonable to conclude that He wants us to know that plan.

Many people object to the belief that God has a specific plan for each of us and wants us to know that plan. They say that sounds too mystical and that we have sufficient intelligence to work out our own destinies. Others say, "Perhaps God does reveal to a few people, such as preachers and missionaries, what He wants them to do by means of some unique experience; but that does not happen to most of us."

The fallacy of that kind of reasoning is that it suggests God has a few special favorites to whom He will reveal a plan for their lives. However, it also would mean that His attitude toward all others is: "I don't really care about you. Do whatever you want with your life." I do not believe that the God we know is that kind of God. Again let me repeat: God has a plan for all of us, and He wants us to know that plan. That leads to the next question: "How does God make known His plan for each of us?"

How We Can Know God's Plan

Very few of us have mystical experiences that include bright lights, bells ringing, and voices that tell us what to do. A common misunderstanding about discovering God's plan is the belief that it will be revealed in some unique, dramatic way or that it must duplicate others' experiences if it is authentic.

Both of these notions are false. God is sovereign, and He will determine the time, place, and manner of revealing His plan for our lives to us. A careful study of the calls of men like Moses (Ex. 3—4), Samuel (1 Sam. 3:2-18), Isaiah (6:1-13), and Ezekiel (1:1—2:8) makes it abundantly clear that they were not seeking to know God's plan. His appearance to them obviously took them by surprise. There is nothing wrong with seeking to know God's plan, but we cannot bring it about, however earnestly we desire to know.

A second fallacy about discovering God's plan is to expect bright lights and earth tremors to accompany the revelation of God's plan for us. But you say, "That's the way Friend X described his experience." Did not God speak to Moses through a burning bush (Ex. 3:1-4)? Did not Ezekiel see bright lights and God seated on a throne (1:26-28)? Wasn't Paul blinded, and didn't he hear the audible voice of Christ (Acts 9:3-4,7-8)? We do not deny the validity of these experiences, but for most of us the discovery of God's plan will be much less spectacular.

God discloses His plan in many different ways. It has been revealed to some while they were reading the Scriptures. How many preachers have discovered God's plan as they read, "How can they hear without someone preaching to them?" (Rom. 10:14)?

God's plan may come into focus during a quiet time of prayer when a strong conviction forms, unaccompanied by dramatic events.

God's plan may become apparent as we are taking inventory of ourselves, our talents, and our interests. I often advise a person who is seeking to know God's plan to consider what he or she would enjoy most if the choices were unlimited. The answer may give a clue, since we are happiest doing what we are best equipped to do.

Aptitude tests and vocational guidance counseling can be helpful. However, they should not be depended on to the exclusion of receiving vocational guidance in other ways from God. While in college I took an aptitude test that showed I should be an architect! That seemed strange, as I had never shown any previous interest in architecture. I later took another test which revealed my interest in mathematics was extremely low; that discovery immediately ruled out architecture. No test or counseling revealed that I should be a preacher or a teacher.

Sometimes a series of circumstances will guide us to the plan that God has ordained for us. Some people refer to circumstantial direction as "open doors" and "closed doors." Sometimes in the absence of a clear-cut sense of direction, all we can do is to pursue a certain opportunity or "open door." At the same time we need to assume an attitude of obedience: "Lord, if this is not the right direction or if it is not what I should do, block it in some unmistakable way."

Three years ago a friend of mine accepted an invitation to teach English in China for one year. He had been seeking some specific way to serve the Lord. The open door to China seemed to be the answer to his prayers. It offered exciting prospects not only for travel and new experiences but also offered an unique opportunity for a Christian witness. At the same time, however, he received an invitation to serve as a director for establishing mission work for a large church in Texas. My friend carefully prayed and chose to go to China. After making all the necessary travel arrangements, he spent the last two weeks visiting family and friends in various parts of the country. However, the day before he was scheduled to fly to China, word came that the Chinese school where he had been invited to teach had hired someone else for the job! The disappointed teacher immediately called the church which had asked him to be its missions director. The church had not hired anyone else for the position and still wanted him to come.

Soon after going to the church he met a lovely young lady with five small children whose husband had been killed in an automobile accident several years earlier. Friendship blossomed into love that culminated in marriage. When I received an invitation to the wedding, I remembered when this friend, in his early thirties, had come to me on several occasions, depressed because it seemed that he was never going to find a wife. When I greeted the couple in the receiving line after the wedding ceremony, I said to the groom, "Now you know why you didn't go to China. The Lord wanted you here to meet the wife He had prepared for you!"

My friend's experience was an example of two doors that were apparently open. Either choice appeared to be a good one. He chose to walk through one that seemed right. It required self-sacrifice, separation from family and friends, and walking into the unknown by faith. However, when that door closed, he accepted it as God's guidance. More of us probably discover God's plan through the trial and error way of open-and-closed doors than through the dramatic "This-is-what-I-want-you-to-do" kind of experience.

Another way that God can reveal His plan for us is through people. God may use a parent, a friend, a pastor, or a teacher to help us discover that plan. Someday in heaven perhaps we will be allowed to know how many people discovered God's plan for their lives through the preaching of an apostle Paul, a John Wesley, a Charles Spurgeon, a Billy Graham, or through something you said or did.

Freedom to Accept or Reject God's Plan

Those with a rigid concept of the sovereignty of God will not agree with my statement that we have the freedom to accept or reject God's plan for us, but I believe that we do. Earlier I stated that God has a plan for us that was determined even before the creation of the world. I believe that is true, but it does not contradict the freedom of choice He has allowed us. That freedom was first revealed to be part of basic human nature in the garden of Eden when the man and woman were given the freedom to obey or disobey God (Gen. 2:16-17). God took an awesome risk when He gave us that freedom—the risk of losing all of us! He could have made us like mechanical robots so that the thought would never enter our heads to disobey Him, but He preferred that our relationship be based on love freely given.

Love cannot be forced; it must always be spontaneous. Suppose a young man is smitten with the girl of his dreams and finally gets the courage to ask her for a date. Her acceptance would send him into orbit, and he would think of nothing but that first date. Suppose, however, when he goes to her home to pick her up, the father meets him at the door with a whip in his hand and says, "Young man, come in. I order you to fall in love with my daughter, and if you don't, I will use this whip on you!" Whatever tender thoughts of love that might have been developing would quickly wither in that young man's heart. He would probably escape out the front door as quickly as possible! In the same way God would never force us to love Him because there could be no true love in such a relationship.

I am further convinced that we have the freedom to accept or reject God's plan because of the number of people who have shared with me their experience of rejecting His plan. I remember vividly a woman in her early fifties who came to me in tears one day to tell me her story.

She was a Sunday School teacher, respected and much loved by everyone in the community. With great emotion she told me that during her teen years she felt that God was calling her to be a missionary, but she rejected the idea, as, in her words, she was having too much fun to give it up to be a missionary.

The years passed, she married, raised a family, and served faithfully in the church. However, she could never forget that she had said no to God's perfect plan for her. Now her age and health made it impossible for her to serve as a foreign missionary, but the memory of what might have been had left a scar in her heart. As she walked away she said, "Whenever you have an opportunity to tell others about my experience, please tell them not to make the same mistake I did."

I came to understand from her experience and others like hers that when we reject God's ideal plan, He does not necessarily throw us on the garbage heap as unusable. Rather, He offers a second plan, not as perfect or as fulfilling as the first but, nevertheless, a meaningful one. For her it was to live an exemplary Christian life before her family and community and to serve as a Sunday School teacher of young people.

God has a plan for each of us. It is good, pleasing, and perfect. It involves the best kind of life we could ever choose to live. It will bring us the greatest amount of satisfaction and happiness, but it requires a willingness to obey God in order to live out that plan.

Principle: God has a plan for each of our lives that will bring us the greatest amount of happiness if we will obey God and accept that plan.

Notes

1. Victor E. Reichert and A. Cohen, "Ecclesiastes," in *The Five Megilloth* (Soncino Books of the Bible), ed. A. Cohen (London: The Soncino Press, 1946), 109.
2. Gary Inrig, *The Hearts of Iron, Feet of Clay* (Chicago: Moody Press, 1979), 111-12.

8
A Command that Will Transform Your Life

Some people have impressive knowledge of the Bible. They can quote verses accurately from any part of it and name the twelve sons of Jacob in chronological order. Others know practically nothing about it. They cannot tell you whether Revelation comes before or after Genesis!

There are, however, two verses so well known that if I stopped passersby at random on a busy street and asked if they could quote a Bible verse, I am sure these two would be quoted. One is John 3:16, that tells how to find life. The other is Matthew 7:12, popularly known as the Golden Rule, that tells how to live life. (Some might cite, "Cleanliness is next to godliness," but hopefully their number would be few!)

A popular proverb says, "Familiarity breeds contempt." It means that we can know someone so well that we no longer appreciate that person's good qualities as we should. I do not mean to suggest that the Golden Rule is so familiar that it is held in contempt. However, familiarity with it can breed indifference. We can quote it so glibly that we never feel any obligation to practice it. Yet it is probably the single most important statement in the Bible that tells how the Christian life should be lived.

Though the verse is well known, it does not follow that it is widely practiced. Also, our application of the Golden Rule is usually quite different from what Jesus had in mind. He was saying that we should treat others as we would like for them to treat us. If we quote it at all, we do so to remind others how they should treat us. When we are mistreated, it is very easy to hurl the Golden Rule at the offender to shame him or her for having mistreated us. However, Jesus' words are stated as a command to us, not as a suggestion: "Do to others what

you would have them do to you." The command says nothing about
the other person's obligation to reciprocate. Therefore, the Golden
Rule should be understood as a mandate for my life and not as a proof
text for the way others should treat me.

A careful analysis of Matt. 7:12 reveals that the verb could be translated, "Keep on doing to others" in spite of how they respond. Also,
the verse is a remarkable summation of the Old Testament (as John
3:16 is a summary of the New Testament). Jesus was saying, "This is
all you need to know about the law and the prophets in the Old
Testament."

An important principle regarding biblical commands is that they
are for our well-being and happiness. None is intended to make us
miserable or to take away life's enjoyment. Since Matthew 7:12 is stated as a command, then we should believe that it is intended for our
good. If we practice it, we will discover a remarkable transformation
taking place within us and in our relationships with others.

If the Golden Rule is commanded, why are we so careless about
practicing it? It is not because it is difficult to understand. Some statements in the Bible are difficult to understand, but not this one. Perhaps the real explanation for our negligence in emphasizing this command is that it is much easier to tell others how to practice
Christianity than to practice it ourselves.

Eavesdrop on a group of Christians, and if you listen long enough,
you will hear someone say, "He should do this," or "She should not
do that." We are quite adept at telling others what they should do.
Our attitude is often like the sweet little lady who arose one day during a controversy at a meeting in the church and said, "If everyone
would just do as I say, everything would be fine." Why don't we hear
more often, "If everyone would just do as I do" rather than "Do as I
say"?

The apostle Paul was not reluctant to say, "I urge you to imitate
me" (1 Cor. 4:16; see Phil. 3:17; 4:9; and 2 Thess. 3:9). Would we be
willing to ask others to pattern their Christian life after ours? Jesus
was aware of our double standard when He warned the people about
their religious leaders: "Do everything they tell you. But do not do
what they do, for they do not practice what they preach" (Matt. 23:3).
The Achilles' heel of many Christians is that we do not practice what

we preach. Recent scandals involving some television evangelists have been a painful and embarrassing reminder of this fact.

All of us would agree that the principle stated in the Golden Rule is good and that we ought to make it the standard for our lives, but few of us make a conscientious effort to practice it. Someone said, "Its simplicity is matched by its difficulty to practice." Our reluctance to risk applying it to our daily living reminds me of pictures I have seen of those intrepid souls who in the midst of winter cut a hole in the ice on the river and challenge each other to be the first to jump in.

We are like them. We encourage others to practice the Christian life, forgetting that there is room for improvement in our own lives. We are quick to advise, "You ought to practice the Golden Rule." Instead, we should say, "I will be the first to put it into practice. I will treat others as I want them to treat me. It does not matter how they treat me. My responsibility is to obey the commands of Jesus before I can ask others to obey them."

I first became aware of my neglect of this commandment while I was serving as a missionary in Brazil. The most eagerly awaited time of day for missionaries is mail delivery. In a foreign country, any communication from back home is welcome. One day I received what appeared to be the kind of letter we are tempted to toss unopened into the wastebasket. You know the kind—a computerized address, third-class postage, and the addressee's name misspelled. However, in a foreign country there were few opportunities to read anything in English, so I opened the envelope to find a small booklet. I'm glad I did because it transformed my understanding of the Golden Rule.

I have since lost the booklet and do not even recall who wrote it, but it was about a man who lived a remarkable life. The booklet described him as an artist, musician, architect, sculptor, and philosopher. He was an intimate friend of great men such as Enrico Caruso, Ignace Paderewski, and Rudyard Kipling. He first became famous when he painted a portrait of the family of President Theodore Roosevelt. He sculpted the likenesses of men such as Thomas Edison and Franklin Roosevelt. He designed and constructed buildings in New York City worth millions of dollars.

I was impressed by this man's genius in so many fields and his acquaintance with so many famous people. But what really caught my attention was the revelation of his "secret" of success. He said, "When I was a child, I resolved to do more for other people than they could do for me, more than they would expect of me, and to do it cheerfully and courteously."[1]

One summer the young man accepted a job as a bellboy in a resort hotel. The salary was $8.00 a month (a large sum for a teenager in those days!), but the manager assured him he would earn $100.00 in tips during the summer. The youth determined not to accept the tips and said to himself: "I'll be the best bellboy the world has ever known. I'll give the most joyful and cheerful service that a bellboy ever gave."

He conscientiously kept his resolution. He arose at 5:00 every morning and never stopped running errands for the guests all day long. If a guest tried to give him a tip, he refused, saying, "I receive a salary, and I love my work." The guests were overwhelmed; they had never met anyone like him. Before the end of the summer, several wealthy families offered to adopt him as their son! That summer the boy established friendships with influential people that lasted a lifetime.

As I thought about this remarkable man, I realized that the "secret" of his life was what I like to call the "amplified version" of the Golden Rule. It was not simply to treat others as he would like to be treated. The man's commitment was to do more for others than they could do for him, do more than was expected or required, and always with a cheerful and courteous attitude.

Transformed Family Relations

What would happen if we practiced the Golden Rule as the bellboy did? Can you imagine how our family relationships would be transformed? What would happen in the home if each member of the family resolved to live by this principle? What would happen if each child does more for the parents and other brothers and sisters than they do for him or her, more than required, and always cheerfully and courteously? It would take time for the parents to recover from the initial shock of having a "new" child, but home would no longer be the battlefield that many homes are.

Husbands often come home from work, tired, out of humor, and wanting to do nothing more than fall on the couch and watch television until bedtime. Even in homes where the wife spends the same number of hours as the husband outside the home working, some husbands expect her to continue with all the household responsibilities—cooking, cleaning, and taking care of the children. What would happen in that kind of home if the husband resolved to do more for his wife than she could do for him? He might come to breakfast some morning and find that the hair curlers and face cream had been removed, and that some of the romance having faded during the years was about to be recaptured.

Wives are probably wanting to rise up and call me blessed for what I have said about husbands, but now let me apply the commandment to the wife. Certainly, in most homes, she already does more for the other members of the family than they do for her. She usually does more than they expect of her, but perhaps a few wives overlook the third part of the advice: do it cheerfully and courteously. Some wives prepare the meals, clean the house, mend the clothes, transport the children to piano lessons, scout meetings, and little league games; but it is a joyless burden to be endured. Life is just one series of Blue Mondays every day of the week. She agrees with an old adage, "Man's work may be from sun to sun, but a woman's work is never done."

One woman complained, "Life is an endless cycle of making beds and washing dishes and then having to do it all over again three hours later!" Tensions on the homemaker can sometimes stretch her to the breaking point, and the result is a shattered home and divorce.

She may choose to be a "liberated" woman, hoping to find fulfillment and happiness in a career. It is possible to find fulfillment and happiness in a career. However, the working wife often discovers that the daily rat race can be just as burdensome and frustrating to her as it is to the working man or to the wife who chooses to remain at home.

Attitude is the all-important key to finding happiness in whatever we do. The most unpleasant task can become bearable and sometimes even enjoyable by a change in attitude. Tests have shown that most fatigue is not due to physical exertion but to dislike of what we are doing. You will never become weary if you are willing to do more for others than they do for you, more than is required, always cheerfully and courteously. Try it for one week and see what happens!

Transformed Church Relations

The church is the one place where we expect relationships to be ideal, but we know they are not. What would happen in a church that practiced the Golden Rule? Most of the disagreements and divisions that plague so many churches would disappear. There would be no such thing as accusations made by some members that other members are favored by the pastor and are given preferred positions in the church. There would be no grumblings of neglect: "The pastor never visits me." "People are not friendly to me." "No one speaks to me." "All they want is my money." Notice how self-centered these complaints are. The unhappiest person in the world is the one who keeps the focus on self. The Golden Rule enables us to focus our attention on others instead of self.

Complaints and discord in the church are not a twentieth-century phenomenon. The Grecian Jews in the early church began complaining against the Aramaic-speaking members that some of their widows were being neglected (Acts 6:1).

What did the church do in that critical situation? It appointed seven men to take care of the members' needs so the apostles could give their time to the ministry of the word of God (Acts 6:2-4). What kind of men were the seven? They could have complained, "Why should we have to take on duties that are not required of everyone?" Instead, they must have been men who were willing to do more for others than others did for them, and they did it voluntarily and lovingly. The dispute was solved because of their willingness to be servants. Most problems in churches today would vanish, especially those involving personal relationships, if we were willing to put others ahead of ourselves.

Much of the activity in churches is nothing more than busy work, confined to the four walls of the church—attending meetings, seminars, and retreats—but never really becoming involved in the outside world where people are hurting. It is easy to keep people at arm's length to avoid getting involved in their problems. At the same time we can greet them warmly on Sunday morning, "We are glad to see you today!"

Why can't we hear the cries of people all around us: "Help me!" "Does anyone care for me?" We will never respond to their appeal unless we are willing to be servants. Most of us do not like to serve others; we had rather be on the receiving end. We prefer not to be reminded that our Lord left an example: "I have set you an example that you should do as I have done for you. I tell you the truth, no servant is greater than his master" (John 13:15-16). What would be the impact of the church on the world today if we became known as "servants"?

Serving does not necessarily mean that we find some glamorous project and devote all our energies to it. We are serving when we visit someone in the hospital, when we take food to a sick friend, clean the house for an elderly neighbor, take care of a young couple's children so they can have an evening out by themselves, or just take time to listen to someone's problems. We may be so busy looking for spectacular ways of serving that we overlook the opportunities that are all around us.

We may be as insensitive as the woman who went to visit a sick friend. She walked past the dirty clothes lying around, did not notice the sink full of dirty dishes, and ignored the two small children crying for their breakfast. She went to the bedside of her sick friend, spoke a few comforting words, and as she walked out, cheerily said, "If there is anything I can do to help, don't hesitate to call on me!"

James had something to say about that kind of person: "Suppose a brother or sister is without clothes and daily food. If one of you says to him, 'Go, I wish you well; keep warm and well fed,' but does nothing about his physical needs, what good is it? In the same way, faith by itself, if it is not accompanied by action, is dead" (2:15-17).

I often hear people say that the church needs to find a new role if it is to survive in today's world that has written it off as irrelevant. I do not believe the church needs to search for a new role. Instead, the church needs to regain her original role: to be salt and light in the world, to be a friend to people in need, to minister to the sorrowing or hurting, to alleviate material needs when we can, and, in short, to be a servant.

"Preaching the Gospel" is more than words spoken from a pulpit on Sunday mornings. "Preaching the Gospel" is living it. Jesus said,

"For I was hungry and you gave me something to eat, I was thirsty and
you gave me something to drink, I was a stranger and you invited me in,
I needed clothes and you clothed me, I was sick and you looked after
me, I was in prison and you came to visit me." Then the righteous will
answer him, "Lord, when did we see you hungry and feed you, or
thirsty and give you something to drink? When did we see you a stranger and invite you in, or needing clothes and clothe you? When did we
see you sick or in prison and go and visit you?" The King will reply, "I
tell you the truth, whatever you did for one of the least of these brothers
of mine, you did for me" (Matt. 25:35-40).

Only if we live the Christian life as servants dedicated to ministering
to the needs of others can we point them to the only Source of a meaningful life—Jesus Christ! When our witnessing is limited to words, a
skeptical world looks at us and says, "Your actions speak so loudly
that I cannot hear what you say." Would it not be better if we could
hear, "Your actions speak so loudly that I am convinced of the truth
of your words"?

Transformed Job Performance

Let's make an application of the "amplified version" of the Golden
Rule to our work: "Do more for our employer than he or she does for
us and more than is expected of us." That is not the attitude of most
employees today, is it? An all-too-common attitude is to do as little as
you can and demand as large a salary as possible. Work as few hours
as you can each week but insist on all the fringe benefits.

I sometimes hear young people say that there are few opportunities
for advancement in today's competitive business world. I think the
reverse is true for the person who would make a commitment to practice the "amplified version" of the Golden Rule. I believe that person
would rise very rapidly, as the employer could not help but be impressed, for so few employees are willing to do more than satisfy the
minimum job requirements.

Some office employees are so skillful that they can give the appearance of working right up to closing time at 5:00. However, they have
been putting things away surreptitiously since 4:50 so that when the
clock strikes five, they can sweep the rest of their papers into their
desk and be on their way out of the building at 5:01. Have you ever

entered a store to make a purchase just before closing time and noticed how unwilling the employees are to wait on you?

Ministers are not exempt from the temptation to "get by." A recent commencement speaker at the seminary where I teach exhorted the graduating class: "Earn what you're paid. There are churches all over America today that are in trouble because they have pastors who suffer from a lack of the Christian work ethic."

Our motive for doing more than the minimum job requirements must not be out of consideration for what we will get in return. That attitude misses the spirit of "doing more for others than they do for you." Some people have advocated the Golden Rule as good business because it made them prosperous. I would not promise (as some have) that your bank account will increase if you practice the Golden Rule, or that people will be appreciative, or that you will win popularity contests. After all, servants are not usually noticed nor paid generous wages. Jesus was the perfect servant and embodiment of the Golden Rule. Yet people responded to Him by nailing Him to a cross. We should not expect better treatment than our Lord received (Matt. 10:24; John 15:20).

Why should we inconvenience ourselves to be servants unless there is something in it for us? A Christian can give only one answer to that question: "Christ's love compels us" (2 Cor. 5:14). We are servants because He commands us to be. The only commendation we desire is His "Well done, good and faithful servant!" (Matt. 25:21). We will experience happiness not found in any other way if we give ourselves unreservedly to being a servant for Christ.

Transformed International Relations

The implications of the Golden Rule are not limited to the home, the church, or the job. What would happen in international relations if nations practiced the "amplified version" of the Golden Rule? Instead of promoting selfish nationalistic interests, nations would seek to help one another without thought of recompense. Instead of aggression and terrorism, there would be love and helpfulness. There would be no grasping for more territory or economic advantage at the expense of other nations. War, hunger, and fear would disappear. The swords could be beaten into plowshares (Isa. 2:4; Mic. 4:3), and an era of peace could be ushered in.

Does that sound too idealistic? Too unrealistic? Yes, as long as nations dare not put the interests of others ahead of their own. As long as the attitude is: "Do to others *before* they do to you," there is no hope for living in harmony and cooperation. Perhaps I am talking about what can only happen when the kingdom of God is finally established. However, isn't it mind boggling to consider how the world could be transformed if all nations would put the well-being of other nations ahead of their own?

What a strange paradox our world is experiencing! At the same time voices crying for world peace become more strident, many of those same voices are determined enemies of the Christian faith. They would like to see it become discredited and disappear from human memory. They refuse to acknowledge that Christ is the only One who can bring world peace because He is the only One who can bring peace to individual hearts (John 14:27). World leaders do not even consider Him in their discussions as they seek solutions for our global tensions which could explode at any moment.

It surely is a confusing age. People put words together in logical sequence with illogical results and yet speak them with all seriousness. They say, "Get rid of Christianity, and leave it to us to produce an ideal world." Sometimes when I hear some of the solutions proposed for our world, I feel a little like Alice in Wonderland when she read the Jabberwocky poem:

> 'Twas brillig,
> and the slithy toves
> did gyre and gimble in the wabe.

Alice concluded, "It seems very pretty, but it's rather hard to understand!" Some of the proposed solutions for our world's problems may sound very pretty, but they will never work because they ignore Christ as the only ultimate solution. In one simple statement, He told us how to solve the specter of nuclear holocaust that haunts us and the unequal distribution of the world's wealth: "In everything, do to others what you would have them do to you."

An Unrealistic Dream?

Dreams of a better world excite us, but we can quickly be brought back to reality if we conclude that the task is hopeless because we are too few to bring it about. However, before we give up we should recall the impact on the first-century world of a handful of men and women whose lives had been touched by Christ. A few committed people can make a difference. We have seen the impact of special-interest groups and lobbyists in our own nation during the past thirty years. Whether we agree with their methods or goals, we must admire their unity and determination to achieve their goals. The Christian community could learn from them—at least we could learn that with a united purpose and commitment we can make a difference.

How can we effectively make an impact on our world? We should first study the early Christians to discover their secret. Theirs was an immoral world. Government policies restricted and persecuted them. They were a small minority, but they began to make a difference.

How did they do it? The answer is obvious if we look for it. It was the way they related to one another. Others began to say in amazement, "See how those Christians love one another." That kind of love was unknown in the carnal, pagan world, but there was something appealing about it. It touched a responsive chord in the heart of the most depraved person. Quietly, without fanfare, unnoticed, like yeast permeating dough, the Christian message began to spread through the Roman Empire. Slaves and the poor and oppressed were drawn to it, as would be expected, but it also reached into the households of the emperor and the nobility.

At the commissioning service for my wife, myself, and twelve other newly appointed missionary couples, the speaker, Dr. Baker James Cauthen, seemed to read our minds as he said, "You are probably wondering how you can make an impact for Christ in the country where you will soon be going. Your greatest contribution will not be your ability to identify with that country's culture. You will always be considered a foreigner. It will not be your ability to speak the language well. You will always make mistakes. Nor will it be the number of churches you build."

By that time all of us were asking ourselves, "Then how can we make an impact in that country?" Before we could find an answer, he continued, "The greatest impact and lasting contribution you can make will be to go to that country, live Christ every day before the people, and love them."

That was good advice for a new missionary. I also believe it is good advice for all Christians, not just for missionaries. The greatest challenge we face is to live each day consistently in front of an unbelieving and skeptical world as Christ would live. That means loving as Christ loves, caring for others, and serving them as He would care and serve. What better way to accomplish this kind of life than to make a commitment to practice the Golden Rule in its "amplified version"?

I am convinced that in the deceptively simple words of Matthew 7:12 Jesus summed up the way the Christian life should be lived. It is the key to living effectively before an unbelieving world. It is the key to living Christianity in a way that is relevant to the complex needs of our world. It is the key to evangelizing the lost. It is also the key to bringing a dimension of happiness to your own life that you never imagined possible. Jesus stated it as a command, not as a suggestion. Therefore, we should obey it.

Try being a servant, and see what happens!

Principle: Our obedience to the Golden Rule will bring happiness to ourselves and to others.

Note

1. My quotations from the booklet may not be exact as I must depend on memory. I have never been able to locate another copy of it.

9

Peace with God as an Essential for Happiness

One of the most remarkable and unique events in all recorded history occurred in February 1985. Yet I did not read about it in any newspaper or newsmagazine or hear it reported on any TV news broadcast. What was it? An obscure trade magazine reported that a peace treaty was signed that month which ended 2,248 years of warfare between Rome and Carthage.[1]

You may be asking, *Have I been asleep? I didn't know Rome was at war, and who or what is a Carthage?* I can't answer the first question for you, but Carthage was one of the great cities of the ancient world, located on the northern African coast at the site of the modern city of Tunis. It was founded in 813 B.C. (sixty years before Rome), and at one time it rivaled Rome in wealth and power. Eventually Rome decided to eliminate Carthage as a threat to her own power in the Mediterranean world. What followed was a series of three wars called the Punic Wars.

The first war lasted from 264 to 241 B.C. and ended with the defeat of Carthage. The second began in 218 B.C. when Hannibal marched his army across the Alps instead of launching a frontal attack from the south. He almost conquered Rome before finally withdrawing in defeat.

In 149 B.C. Rome determined to destroy her ancient rival once and for all. Spurred by Cato's repeated cry in the Roman Senate, *"Delenda est Carthago"* ("Carthage must be destroyed"), Rome sent an army that laid siege to Carthage. After a fierce struggle, Carthage surrendered and was leveled to the ground by the Romans. They buried the ruins under twenty-two feet of rubble and spread salt over the ground so nothing could ever grow there again. Its total destruction has been called the Hiroshima of antiquity.

However, no peace treaty was signed to end the war between the two ancient foes until February 1985, when the mayors of Rome and Tunis met in a formal ceremony to sign a peace treaty. Thus a war was officially brought to an end that had begun 2,248 years earlier!

When I read the account of the signing of the peace treaty, my first thought was: *What a commentary on the human race!* We have been at war with God not for 2,248 years, but ever since the beginning of human history. No peace treaty has ever been signed because humankind as a whole is still in rebellion against God's rule. The prophet Isaiah said,

> The wicked are like the tossing sea,
> which cannot rest,
> whose waves cast up mire and mud.
> "There is no peace," says my God,
> "for the wicked" (57:20-21).

Our refusal to accept God's sovereignty and to acknowledge His Son amounts to a declaration of war against God. Furthermore, the Scriptures warn that every person who remains in rebellion against God is under His judgment (Eph. 5:6; 1 Pet. 4:5; and Rev. 20:11-15).

Dr. Robert Oppenheimer, who supervised the production of the first atomic bomb exploded during World War II, was called before a congressional committee hearing. He was asked if there was any defense against the bomb. Oppenheimer's reply was, "Certainly." Pressed further with the question: "What is it?" he answered in one word: "Peace." The same kind of question could be asked: Is there any defense against God's judgment? The answer would be: "Certainly! Make peace with God."

God Wants Peace with Us

It is not God's desire that we be His enemies. He has demonstrated repeatedly that He wants to make peace with us. When the first rebellion occurred in the garden of Eden, God punished the man and the woman and drove them from the garden. However, in a gesture that showed His desire for reconciliation and His continuing love, He provided them with garments of animal skins (Gen. 3:21).

When wickedness on the earth became so widespread that every thought of men and women was evil all the time, God destroyed the earth by a flood. However, instead of destroying the human race completely, He spared one family and made a vow never to destroy the earth again by water (Gen. 6:1—9:17). Thus, the way to reconciliation was kept open.

At Mount Sinai God again showed His desire for reconciliation by making a covenant with the recently liberated Israelite slaves. It was a covenant that was based on their willingness to obey His commands (Ex. 19:5-6).

The birth of Jesus was the climactic evidence of God's desire for peace with the human race He had created. On the night of Jesus' birth, the angels announced: "Glory to God in the highest, and on earth peace to men on whom his favor rests" (Luke 2:14). Shortly before His arrest and death, Jesus comforted His disciples with these words: "Peace I leave with you; my peace I give you. I do not give to you as the world gives. Do not let your hearts be troubled and do not be afraid" (John 14:27). After His resurrection, His first words to the gathered disciples were: "Peace be with you!" (Luke 24:36; John 20:19).

Paul's encounter with the risen Christ on the Damascus Road made a lasting impression on him regarding the peace with God he experienced through Christ. He wrote to the Romans: "Since we have been justified through faith, we have peace with God through our Lord Jesus Christ" (Rom. 5:1). Paul began each of his thirteen letters with the salutation: "Grace and peace" and added, "from God our father" or "from God the father" to each of his greetings.

The Bible has sometimes been described as the story of humankind's search for God, but a more thoughtful examination reveals that it is the story of humankind's flight from God and God's efforts to bring us back to Him. He wants to be our friend. Jesus made a poignant appeal to Jerusalem for its friendship: "O Jerusalem, Jerusalem, you who kill the prophets and stone those sent to you, how often I have longed to gather your children together, as a hen gathers her chicks under her wings, but you were not willing" (Matt. 23:37). On another occasion He pleaded for reconciliation: "Come to me, all you who are weary and burdened, and I will give you rest" (Matt. 11:28).

God's Initiative in Making Peace

In warfare the defeated foe ordinarily takes the initiative in seeking terms of peace with the victor. Human history does not reveal, however, that we have taken the initiative in making peace with God. Rather, hiding from God has characterized us since the first man and woman hid from God after refusing to obey His command concerning the forbidden fruit (Gen. 3:8).

God took the initiative to make a covenant with Israel at Mount Sinai. A principal condition of that covenant was that they would worship no other gods, to which they agreed (Ex. 20:3-6; 24:3). Unfortunately, their subsequent history proved the insincerity of their commitment. Even while still camped at Mount Sinai, the children of Israel made a golden calf and began to worship it (Ex. 32:1-6).

Almost forty years later, in spite of their repeated acts of rebellion along the way, God brought them to the Promised Land. But even while camped on the east side of the Jordan River and shortly before entering the land, the people were enticed by the Moabites to worship Baal of Peor, a storm god (Num. 25:1-3).

After occupying the land, the people continued to worship other gods. Just before his death, Joshua appealed to them: "Throw away the gods your forefathers worshiped beyond the River and in Egypt, and serve the Lord" (Josh. 24:14, see Ezek. 20:5-8). Centuries later on Mount Carmel, Elijah challenged the people to make a choice: "How long will you waver between two opinions? If the Lord is God, follow him; but if Baal is God, follow him" (1 Kings 18:21).

During the period of the Israelite monarchy not only did the people worship other gods, but their kings also gave their allegiance to the idols (2 Kings 16:4). They openly "set up sacred stones and Asherah poles on every high hill and under every spreading tree" (2 Kings 17:10).

God warned the people time and again through the prophets to turn from their evil ways (2 Kings 17:13). Hosea appealed: "Return, O Israel, to the Lord your God. Your sins have been your downfall!" (Hos. 14:1). Through the prophet Jeremiah, God repeatedly appealed to the people to return to Him (3:12,14,22; 4:1). After all the warnings had been ignored, Jerusalem was destroyed, and many of the people were carried into Exile; but they were still not disposed to seek God. After their return from Exile, nothing had changed. God had to appeal through the prophet Malachi (around 460 B.C.): "Return to me, and I will return to you" (Mal. 3:7).

All the appeals, warnings, and punishment were ineffective in bringing about reconciliation between God and Israel. Therefore, He sent His Son last of all, saying: "They will respect my son" (Mark 12:6). But Jesus anticipated in a parable that would not be the case. Instead, they would take the son and kill him as a final defiant act to establish their independence from God's sovereign authority (Mark 12:8; see John 1:11). Even while hanging on the cross, Jesus continued to seek reconciliation as He prayed, "Father, forgive them, for they do not know what they are doing" (Luke 23:34).

Every page of human history to the present time is a continuation of the same story—humankind's ongoing rebellion against God and God's unchanging desire to make peace.

An analogy may help us appreciate God's remarkable patience with us in seeking reconciliation. Suppose the state of Utah decided to declare war on the rest of the United States without weapons of any kind, whereby it could win the war. With our stockpile of atomic and hydrogen bombs, the nation's military forces could crush the revolt in a matter of minutes if they chose to do so. The rebels should be the ones to take the initiative to sue for peace in order to avoid total destruction, but they refuse to do so. Instead of resorting to force, however, the nation's leaders seek a voluntary return with generous terms of forgiveness and abundant gifts.

That does not sound like the scenario of any human warfare, does it? Yet, that is the way God has chosen to make peace with us. He could destroy the human race (as He did once before in the time of Noah). Instead, He has chosen to take the initiative to bring about reconciliation. The terms are all in our favor—complete forgiveness and receiving the status of children and joint heirs (Rom. 8:17; Gal. 4:7; Titus 3:5-7; and James 2:5). We are required to do only one thing to obtain that relationship: accept Christ as our Lord and Savior through faith.

Peace Is Made on God's Terms

The Scriptures make it clear that peace with God can be achieved only on the terms God has laid down. Romans 5:1-2 states those terms unambiguously: "We have peace with God through our Lord Jesus Christ, through whom we have gained access by faith into this grace in which we now stand." Jesus emphatically stated, "I am the way and the truth and the life. No one comes to the Father except through me" (John 14:6).

God has provided no other means for reconciliation. Therefore, Christians should be unapologetic in proclaiming Jesus as the only way to peace with God. There is an ecumenical spirit abroad which is unwilling to insist that faith in Christ is the only way of salvation. We need to be reminded that the early church was not reluctant to proclaim a "one-way-only" salvation. Peter, filled with the Holy Spirit, said, "Salvation is found in no one else, for there is no other name under heaven given to men by which we must be saved" (Acts 4:12). Well-intentioned ecumenism, with its understandable desire to avoid offending anyone, actually does a disservice to those persons who are alienated from God by suggesting that there are any number of ways for making peace with God.

During the darkest days of World War II, the Allied nations jointly announced terms of unconditional surrender for the enemy. That meant there would be no gathering around a peace table to discuss the terms of peace, as was done at Versailles at the end of World War I. The enemy would be allowed no voice in determining the terms on which peace would be established. If the Allied powers had not been able to prove their military superiority, their announced terms of unconditional surrender would have been a farce. If a stalemate could have been achieved by the enemy, negotiations would have been required before peace could have been realized.

God has announced terms of unconditional surrender to a world at war with Him. But when we surrender to Him, He does not make slaves of us or take everything away from us in order to punish us. Instead, He receives us as the father received his prodigal son—with joy and celebration (Luke 15:22-24). God accepts us as His sons and daughters and blots out our rebellious past. Surrender to an enemy is considered to be the worst calamity that could happen to a nation, but surrender to God is the best thing that could ever happen to any person.

Though terms of unconditional surrender were announced during World War II, the victorious Allies did not impose harsh, crippling terms on the enemy as they had done at the end of World War I. Instead, our country adopted the Marshall Plan and sent millions of dollars in massive aid to help rebuild the defeated nations. As evidence of the generosity of the aid given, Germany and Japan today enjoy two of the strongest economies in the world. In the same way, God's "Marshall Plan" becomes operative when we make peace with Him on His terms and become the recipients of His blessings.

The Desirability of Peace with God

Some would argue that the worst decision we could make would be to yield control of our lives to God. Many have been deceived into believing that acknowledging the lordship of Christ will take all pleasure out of life when the reverse is true. Jesus promised an abundant life (John 10:10, "to the full"). The fruit of the Holy Spirit is "love, joy, peace" (Gal. 5:22). To quote a popular TV auto commercial: "Who could ask for anything more?"

What exactly is "peace" with God? The Old Testament word is *shalom.* It includes the idea of absence of warfare, but it is much more than that. *Peace* is an all-inclusive word that suggests wholeness and well-being, that is, everything that life should be. It can include bodily health, material prosperity, and stability of relationships. The New Testament word for "peace" is *eirene* (from which our word *irenic* comes). Its meaning is much the same as the Old Testament word and also includes the idea of salvation.[2]

When we experience peace with God, something happens that is described variously as "new birth," "regeneration," or becoming a "new creation." No single word can adequately describe everything that happens when we yield to God, but the transformation is genuine.

At a church in Brazil where I once served as pastor, a motorcycle gang decided to disrupt our Sunday morning services by riding up and down the street in front of the church. The noise of their motors was so loud that we were forced to stop the service until the gang decided they had had enough "fun."

One Sunday morning, however, after several weeks of disrupting our services, one of their gang, wearing a black leather jacket, entered the church and sat in a pew near the back. Some were concerned that the young man had come to disrupt the service, but he left quietly at its conclusion. The next Sunday he returned and continued returning week after week. Each Sunday the motorcyclist moved closer to the front until he was only a few rows from the pulpit.

It was a slight blow to my preacher ego (that assumed he was attracted by my preaching!) when I learned that his only reason for attending our services was to impress a young lady who sang in the choir to whom he was attracted. However, as he attended each Sunday, he began to listen to the messages from the pulpit and became persuaded that he wanted to become a Christian.

One Sunday morning after the service the young man approached me in the church's foyer and asked if he could talk to me. I ushered him into an adjoining room, certain that he wanted to make inquiry about how to become a Christian. However, some of the deacons who had observed us going into the room concluded that the youth was going to attack an unsuspecting preacher and rob him, so six of them (unknown to me) gathered outside the door. One had his ear against the door, and all of them were prepared to burst in to rescue me at the first sound of foul play!

I was unaware that the men were gathered outside the door as the two of us sat down to talk. In a few minutes the motorcyclist began to weep and to pray for Christ's forgiveness and salvation. When he ended his prayer, I think I have never witnessed such an immediate transformation in the countenance of a person as I saw in his. It was as though the tears had washed away the hardened, cruel look on his face, replacing it with a countenance of serenity and happiness. There was no other way to explain what was happening except that the youth had experienced peace with God.

We opened the door to leave and encountered the men standing there poised to rescue me. As soon as they saw his face, without asking, they realized what had happened and began weeping and hugging him. The young man became a faithful member of the church and never returned to his motorcycle gang, as he had found something better.

I do not believe that every person who makes peace with God will experience a physical transformation, but it should not be surprising when it does happen. The face is a true mirror of the soul. It reveals the inner feelings to the careful observer (Prov. 15:13; Neh. 2:2-3). When a person is angry, depressed, worried, fearful, or confused, the face frequently reveals those emotions. When a person is happy, at peace with self and with God, freed from the guilt of sin, and with a new sense of purpose and meaning, it should not be surprising that what he or she feels within is noticeable to others.

If you have ever attended a high-school class reunion, you know it can be an experience that is both enjoyable and traumatic. Even though you know you have not aged (!), you may see the wrinkled faces and graying hair of friends and feel emotionally shaken by their changed appearance. I attended a reunion of my high-school class several years ago and experienced the same kind of shock. It seemed that some friends had not changed at all. Others were unrecognizable until they told me their names.

I saw one close friend from high school and college days across the room at the same time he saw me. We walked toward each other, but I was not prepared for his greeting. He looked at me intently for a moment and said, "F. B., you look like you are really happy with your life." He knew that I had given up a business career to enter the ministry at the same time he was establishing himself in his chosen profession. I am sure he never understood my sudden change in careers.

As I looked at my old friend, I realized that he had achieved the goals we had both shared earlier—to be a success socially, professionally, and materially. I was unable to tell him that he appeared to be happy, for it would not have been true. He was tense and unable to smile. Though he had achieved all the goals he had earlier established and that most people would covet, the man had not found happiness.

Warfare between nations is destructive, costly to all who are involved in it, and no one is really a winner. It brings out the worst in human nature: greed, cruelty, and violence. It wastes natural resources, but more importantly it wastes human resources. I have sometimes wondered how many potential Einsteins, Beethovens, Lincolns, and Billy Grahams have been sacrificed to Mars, the god of war.

While a high-school student, I was first introduced to a poem that made a lasting impression on me for its beauty. The poem, written by Joyce Kilmer, was called "Trees." Kilmer had a remarkable love for the common and beautiful things in the world and was able to express his feelings about them in simple, yet touching ways. He was killed in action in France in 1918 at the age of thirty-two, just a few months before World War I ended. I have sometimes wondered what other beautiful poetry he might have written, had he lived.

If human warfare is destructive, costly, and wasteful, how much more is spiritual warfare! Those persons who refuse to make peace with God will never realize the full potential of their lives. They will continue to search and never understand what is missing. They will never know inner well-being and wholeness that comes from reconciliation with God. All of us know the good feeling that comes when we make up with a friend after an argument. That "good feeling" is even more profound when we "make up" with God.

Readers old enough to remember August 14, 1945 (August 15, Tokyo time), will never forget the uninhibited euphoria of that day when World War II finally came to an end. There was dancing in the streets and celebrations, large and small, all over the world that lasted through the night. Peace had finally come after the most destructive and widespread war in human history. But the unbridled joy of that day cannot equal the explosion of happiness we experience when we make peace with God.

How Is Peace with God Achieved?

If God wants peace with us, takes the initiative to establish it, and it is the best thing that could ever happen to us, how do we obtain it?

There is only one answer: through the obedience of faith in Jesus Christ we have peace with God. Why do I say "through the obedience of faith" rather than simply "through faith"? I intentionally stated it that way because to have peace with God requires our willingness to obey Him by accepting salvation in the manner He has provided. If we continue to insist that there are many ways of being reconciled to God other than by faith in Christ, then we are being disobedient to God and will remain alienated from Him.

Faith requires submission, and submission comes through obedience. Once again we have seen that obedience is the key to happiness, for we cannot be truly happy until we have made peace with God.

Principle: Human happiness is fully experienced only when we have peace with God through the obedience of faith in Jesus Christ.

Notes

1. Paul Lunde, "Delenda est Carthage," *Aramco World* 36 (May-June 1985): 18-25.
2. Werner Foerster and Gerhard von Rad, *"eirene,"* in *Theological Dictionary of the New Testament,* ed. Gerhard Kittel (Grand Rapids, Wm. B. Eerdmans Publishing Co., 1964): 2:400-20.

10

The Lordship of Christ and Your Happiness

Can Christ be Savior and not be Lord of our lives? Answers to this question do not always agree. Some say that unless we yield in obedient submission to His lordship, we have not really made Him Savior. They believe the two commitments must be simultaneous.

Others say Christ becomes both Savior and Lord when we are converted, but only with the maturing of our faith do we begin to understand all that was involved in the conversion experience. As we do, we begin to obey Him as Lord.

Still others say that acceptance of Christ as Savior and Lord are two separate decisions, and that the distinction should not be blurred. Since the commitment to Christ as Savior was the result of a crisis experience in which we recognized our sins and our need for forgiveness, they say we will come to an acknowledgment of Christ as Lord as a result of another crisis experience.

Even as we must beware of insisting that every conversion experience be identical, so we must not insist that acceptance of Christ's lordship comes in the same way to every believer.

Both Savior and Lord at Conversion

Some new Christians have a good grasp of Christ both as Savior and Lord of their lives from the moment of conversion. Their obedience from the very beginning is admirable. They do not seem to have a struggle to put away the practices of the old life that some of us do. It is true that from the moment we accept Christ as Savior we die to self (Gal. 2:20), but some give evidence that the old self appears to be alive and well. How do we explain the apparent contradiction between what the Scriptures say we have become and what we actually experience?

An analogy can serve as an answer for this troubling question. Have you ever killed a snake? It is not a pleasant task, but the surest way to deal the death blow is to cut off its head. The snake is quite dead but continues to wiggle for some time, giving all the appearances of life. In fact, an old saying in my part of the country is that the snake does not stop wiggling until sundown, regardless of the time of day you chop off its head!

Mark, a friend of mine, is a remarkable example of a new Christian who accepted the lordship of Christ without a period of resistance. Mark was a political science major in college, a brilliant student who studied five languages. He had a distinguished army career after college, serving in the Green Berets in Vietnam. Converted at age twenty-four, Mark studied and received his law degree and practiced law until age thirty-one, then he gave up his law career as soon as he experienced God's call to be a foreign missionary.

After completing three years of seminary study, Mark took his wife and three children to Guatemala to serve as missionaries living among the Indians in very primitive conditions.

A letter I received from Mark sums up his spirit of submission to Christ's lordship: "I cannot forget that moment nearly twelve years ago when Jesus Christ changed my life. From that day He has been consuming it. There could exist a no more unlikely candidate to be sent to God's creation: the Quiche people. The bottom line is that Jesus is everything I have. Little by little other things are being stripped away."

This kind of Christian merits our respect and admiration, but not all of us can say that from the moment of conversion Jesus totally consumed our wills.

Acknowledging Christ's Lordship as a Process

Most Christians arrive at an acceptance of the lordship of Christ as a result of a maturing process. There are many things we do not understand about the Christian faith when we first become Christians. Peter calls us "newborn babies" (1 Pet.. 2:2). It is a good analogy.

From the moment of birth that baby is your child, and you are its parent. Nothing can change that physical relationship. However, your parental relationship will change as the child grows and matures. When a baby first says "Ma-ma" or "Da-da," it has only a faint understanding of what those words mean. Later the child will learn that "Ma-ma" and "Da-da" require more than a smile now and then. The child will learn that he or she must obey the parents.

Sometimes a child who has been quite obedient transforms into a monster when the teen years are reached. Suddenly the formerly docile, agreeable child begins to assert his or her independence, sometimes in a way that is obnoxious, deliberately doing things to irritate the parents.

Even a child who became a Christian in the preteens may reject all the Christian teachings learned in the earlier years. Teen alcohol and drug abuse along with premarital sex are not limited to non-Christian youth by any means. If you believe that they are, let me sell you the Brooklyn Bridge at a real bargain!

Sometimes during those difficult years of rebellion, parents can only hope and pray that "this, too, will pass" and that the child will once again embrace the faith from which he or she has strayed (Prov. 22:6).

Unfortunately, some children never stop breaking their parents' hearts. Several years ago I was leading a Bible study in a church in a nearby city. A white-haired lady in her seventies approached me after the Monday evening study to tell me that she and her husband would not be able to attend the study the following evening, whereupon she began to weep. I was not egotistical enough to think she was weeping because she would miss my Bible study, so I waited until she was able to continue speaking. She explained, "Our son, age forty-six, is a hopeless alcoholic confined to a hospital, and we go to visit him every Tuesday night."

At a time of life when parents should be enjoying the satisfaction of seeing their children living their own lives successfully, this couple only knew the heartbreak of a son who would never be a blessing to them in their advanced years (see Prov. 10:1). If parents can feel such intense grief for a child who has wrecked the potential of his life, how much more must God suffer for our waywardness.

It is easy to call Christ "Lord" or "Master," but it often takes years before He really is. Through the prophet Malachi God reminded the people that a servant knew that he should honor his master. God accused the Israelites of calling Him "Master" but not giving Him the honor due a master (Mal. 1:6.) Jesus similarly asked, "Why do you call me , 'Lord, Lord,' and do not do what I say?" (Luke 6:46).

Acceptance of Christ's Lordship through Crisis

There is still another way by which Christians come to accept the lordship of Christ, and that is through a crisis experience. A situation may arise that requires a definite decision: either Christ will truly become Lord, or the rest of life may be spent in the halfway house of the Christian faith—sometimes obeying, sometimes rebelling.

I came to understand Christ's claim of lordship through crisis. I was converted at age twenty-four after an intensely painful four-months' struggle of wanting Christ as Savior, but not wanting Him. Shortly after that decision was settled, He tested me to see if I was ready to acknowledge His lordship by calling me to the ministry. I wasn't ready, for it took another six years before I made that decision and began seminary training. During the three years of seminary studies there was another conflict, as a result of God's additional clarification of my ministry—to serve as a foreign missionary—before I reluctantly acknowledged that this was what I must do.

When I and my family boarded a boat for Brazil to begin our missionary service, I am sure all my friends thought I was 100-percent yielded to the lordship of Christ. How much more committed can one be than by becoming a foreign missionary? I am sure some friends could see a halo shining brightly above my head, but in my heart I knew better.

I actually set out for Brazil angry at God for "forcing" me to be a foreign missionary. He simply would not leave me alone and let me have a life of my own choosing.

I arrived in Brazil with my heels firmly dug into the ground. My attitude was,"Now, Lord, are You satisfied? You made me miserable until I became a missionary. Get off my back now and let me enjoy some peace!" I had never changed my opinion that God should have let me live my life the way I had planned it. I had wanted to remain in my hometown where I had grown up and stay in the business where I was comfortably established. I did not want to give up the familiar surroundings of family and friends. Even after becoming a Christian, I was willing to make only minor adjustments in my life's plans. I was willing to be a Christian laywitness-businessman but no more. Now there is nothing wrong with being a Christian laywitness-businessman—we need more of them! But that was not what God had planned for my life.

We had been in Brazil about four months when our then two-year-old son was stricken with a tropical virus. For five days his temperature hovered around 105 degrees. He was rapidly dehydrating and getting weaker. We took him to several local doctors, as sick as he was (they did not make house calls), but none could diagnose the illness.

It was apparent that the child could not survive many more days in that condition. At the same time inside of me a spiritual sickness was raging that was as severe as my son's physical illness. I was fuming against God, "I guess You are satisfied now, God. You forced me to come to Brazil in order to take David from us." I knew, of course, that our children could have contracted a serious or fatal disease in the States, but at least they could have been given the best medical attention possible, whereas David was getting none at all.

After almost a week with no change in David's condition, around 11:00 one night after the last Brazilian friend had left, my wife and I knelt together to pray before retiring to try to get a little rest. In my rebellious state it seemed as if the blackness and gloom of the night was pressing in on me from every side as I began to pray. I really was not prepared for the words I spoke, however. Emotionally drained, I found myself saying, "Lord, I don't understand why You are taking David from us, but I have to trust You regardless of whatever may happen." It was a prayer of desperation and release.

The next morning a Brazilian friend telephoned and recommended that we take David to a doctor whom she knew; she felt sure that he could help. After a brief examination, the doctor said, "I know what the virus is, and I know how to treat it." He gave us a prescription, and in a day or two the fever had broken, and David was beginning to recover.

As I have thought about that crisis many times since, I realized that in a moment of desperation, when I did not know what else to do, I finally accepted the absolute lordship of Christ. I finally believed that

I had to trust—that I could trust Him—regardless of what happened. From that day to this I have never looked back to wish that I could have lived out my life as I had planned it. I do not mean to imply that my obedience has always been 100 percent (the old dead self still wiggles now and then!). However, I have never desired to live any other life than the one I now enjoy. In fact, I sometimes wonder why I was so stubbornly reluctant and so slow to believe that the will of God is "good, pleasing and perfect' (Rom. 12:2).

E. Stanley Jones, the best-known Methodist missionary of the twentieth century, also came to the lordship of Christ through crisis. He wrote, "I find my spiritual life getting on by a series of crises, each lifting to a higher level, and each the precursor of larger demands on me."[1]

Jones described a period of his life when he was experiencing an intense hunger for more of God as a young law student. As he prayed, it seemed a Voice said, "Will you give Me your all?" Without hesitation Jones replied, "Yes, Lord." He was surprised that the Voice responded, "Then take My all."

When Jones announced to his mother that he was giving up law for the ministry, she exclaimed, "What, a poor Methodist preacher!" Jones commented, "She was willing for me to be converted, but not too far!"

Later he experienced a call to be a foreign missionary, but the decision proved to be too much for Jones's mother. She had difficulty accepting his call to the ministry, but she was crushed to think about his going to a faraway country. He received a telegram from his brother to come home immediately, for his mother was dying. On the way he felt the accuser telling him that he had killed his mother. Jones knew he had to make a decision. He could yield to his mother's will so she would live, or he could fulfill God's will and be the cause of her death.

When he arrived home, Jones was told that the cause of his mother's illness could not be determined. She had lost the will to live. But Jones knew. He also knew that he had to obey God's will, whether his mother lived or died.

When he made that irrevocable decision, to everyone's amazement Jones's mother recovered and lived for several more years. Her spiritual perception had changed, also. Just before she died, she said, "Do not put a crepe upon the door, put a bunch of white flowers instead; and do not lay me out in black, dress me in white, for it will be my coronation day—the happiest day of my life, for I shall be with Him."

Jones concluded as a result of that crisis that if we acknowledge the lordship of Christ, we can safely entrust every situation in life to Him. He later commented, "There will be many more crises to come, each leading to a higher conversion and call. Life with Christ is a beautiful adventure. 'It doesn't take much of a man to be a Christian, but it takes all there is of him.' But then we get all there is of Him."

Through crisis E. Stanley Jones found that obedience which results in acknowledging the lordship of Christ is the only way to find genuine happiness and fulfillment.

The usual emphasis on the Great Commission (Matt. 28:19-20) is on the "go," but the only imperative in the Greek language in these verses is: "make disciples." All the other key verbs are participating—going, "baptizing," and "teaching." The participles describe what is essential in order to make disciples. We must "go" find them, as they will not come to us. Baptizing is the way that Christ has chosen for us to identify openly with Him (Rom. 6:3-4). Teaching enables the new disciple to understand his or her Master and what is expected of one who is a declared follower of Christ.

What is it that we are to teach a new disciple? We do not have to look beyond the Great Commission to find the answer. Jesus said, Teach "them to obey ["observe," KJV] everything I have commanded you" (Matt. 28:20). If we disciple according to Christ's instructions, we will teach the new convert the absolute necessity of obeying Christ's commands. Only then does that new Christian who knows Christ as Savior begin to know Him as Lord.

Principle: Acceptance of the lordship of Christ depends on our willingness to obey Him.

Note

1. E. Stanley Jones, *Christ at the Round Table* (New York: Grosset and Dunlap Publisher, 1928): 86. This quotation and the rest of Jones's story that follows are found on pp. 86-89.

11
A Neglected Requirement for Happiness

Historians will look back on the twentieth century as the time of greatest change ever in human history. Scientific, technological, political, sociological, and cultural changes have created a new world hardly recognizable by anyone who lived in the nineteenth century. But the greatest change, more like a revolution, has taken place in the arena of morality.

During World Wars I and II, hundreds of thousands of men experienced freedom from the moral restraints exercised by their home communities. When these men returned from overseas, they were unwilling to return to the old, stricter standards. Traditional moral codes began to soften during the first half of the twentieth century, although most people were not aware of what was taking place.

Suddenly, in the 1960s the moral revolution exploded, challenging and rejecting the moral codes that had been largely accepted for centuries.

Murder, violence, terrorism, and every kind of immorality increased in alarming, uncontrollable proportions. Drug dealers had no pangs of conscience for the millions of lives they were destroying with the wares they peddled. As long as they made a profit, nothing else was important. People openly ridiculed the moral codes that had governed previous generations. The Ten Commandments could not even be posted on school room walls. The only criterion became, "If it makes you feel good, do it."

Living together without benefit of marriage was no longer stigmatized. Men and women shared the same college dormitories. Women who conceived children out of wedlock were no longer called "ruined" women, including many famous figures in the entertainment world. Casual sex replaced the good-night kiss. Nudity (Remember "streakers"?) and sexual orgies became commonplace. Marijuana, LSD, and other mind-altering drugs, though illegal, found widespread acceptance. Sexually explicit books, magazines, and films that formerly would have been read or viewed in secret are now protected against the threat of censorship as part of our constitutional rights. Casual conversation between men and women now includes talk about sex that would have made a previous generation blush, or, at least, it would have been limited to the locker room. Dishonesty, immorality, and corruption in business and government have become commonplace since the 1960s moral revolution began.

Moral conduct that was formerly accepted without question is being called into question and rejected. Practices that formerly were considered unacceptable and actually harmful are now defended as being right. No one has ever better expressed the moral flip-flop that began in the 1960s than the prophet Isaiah over 2700 years ago:

> Woe to those who call evil good
> and good evil,
> who put darkness for light
> and light for darkness,
> who put bitter for sweet
> and sweet for bitter (Isa. 5:20)

Even segments of the church became involved in promoting and legitimizing the new morality. As reported in *Time*, in October 28, 1966, the British Council of Churches published a report on "Sex and Morality" in which it rejected the Christian case for purity before marriage and faithfulness within marriage. It refused to endorse the biblical condemnation of fornication, which it felt was permissible in some situations. Some churches have officially sanctioned homosexuality as an acceptable alternate life-style. Sexual indiscretion is more common among Christians than we like to admit. Even the clergy are not exempt. However, they often are quickly forgiven by their congregation for moral indiscretions because many of them are doing the same thing.

So-called Christian leaders got into the act and encouraged the "new morality." Some of them began crusading during the sixties on behalf of sexual perversion, topless burlesque dancers, and marriage-less unions. Other church leaders became advocates of the "God is dead" movement. With God out of the way and no ultimate account-ability of a final Judgment Day, there were no apparent reasons for further restraint. One concerned radio preacher said, "Who lives his life as if God is a reality today?"

Conservative Christians were so traumatized by the new morality and so certain it would be abandoned when cooler heads prevailed that little was done at first to counteract the trend. Christian efforts were largely limited to appeals from the pulpit (but their audiences were already in agreement with them; those who disagreed had al-ready left the church) and to bumper-sticker warfare. Automobiles of Christians began sprouting fish insignias (though drivers often belied by the way they drove that they were Christians!) and bumper-sticker slogans such as: "My God is not dead—sorry about yours!" Others took comfort from the belief that the rapture would soon lift them out of the morass, so why fight it? Some Christians were sure that the whole thing was a bad dream that would go away if they just contin-ued to sleep long enough.

A careful analysis of reasons for the violent resistance to the new Christian faith in the first century reveals that one of the main factors was its condemnation of the immorality so prevalent in the Roman Empire (1 Pet. 4:3-4). When we are doing wrong, we will either allow our consciences to convict us, or we will deny the wrong and attempt to stifle the source of the troubled conscience (see Amos 2:12; 5:10; Mic. 2:11; and Luke 13:34). If the early Christians had conformed, there would have been no persecution and no martyrs, but in a few years there would have been no Christian witness! If Christianity dis-appears as a major religious and moral force in the next century, it will not be because we stubbornly insist on being "different," but it will be because of our willingness to conform to the world's standards.

The revolt was not limited to morals. So complete was it that the generation of the 1960s rejected anything that had been commonly acceptable behavior and practice up to that time. If the previous gen-eration bathed, the new one would not. If the previous generation shaved, the new one would grow beards. If the previous generation wore shoes, this one would go barefoot. If the previous generation dressed neatly and modestly, the "now" generation would wear faded, torn jeans or miniskirts. If profanity had been limited to the locker room, the vocabulary of the "now" generation would be largely composed of four-letter words casually spoken in mixed groups without embarrassment (see Jer. 6:15; 8:12).

What Has the New Morality Accomplished?

The new morality has been around long enough that its effects on our society can be studied. The question now needs to be raised: Has it really produced a better world? Has the Age of Aquarius arrived?

One does not have to be a Christian to know that an honest answer to that question is an unqualified no! Our nation enjoys affluence and freedom such as no other people has ever experienced. Others look enviously at us and are convinced that if they had what we have, they would be happy. But we are not a happy people. The message of liberation from all moral restraints that was touted as the way to happiness has not delivered what it promised. Utopia has not arrived. The eighties have come and gone. Instead, we have experienced an intensification of dissatisfaction, crime, violence, suicide, greed, dishonesty, terrorism, venereal diseases, child abuse, fear, ugliness, and unhappiness such as no other generation has even known.

What was hailed as something new and exciting ("innovative" and "creative" were popular shibboleths) was not so new after all (Eccl. 1:10). The rebellion of the sixties was motivated by the same temptation that appealed to the first man and woman: "Rebel against God, and you will become God."[1] Adam and Eve discovered that their revolt did not give them what it promised, and today's moral rebellion will not deliver what it promises, either.

I have frequently pondered the question: Why have Christians been hated and persecuted through the centuries? If the world were truly Christian, there would be universal peace and love. There would be equitable distribution of the world's goods. There would be no mistreated or oppressed people anywhere. There would be no crime, brutality, violence, terrorism, corruption in government, dishonest business practices, or mistreatment of any human being. Isn't this the kind of world people want to live in? If so, why have Christians been hated, ridiculed, and persecuted, even to the present day?

I do not believe that the rejection of Christ is caused by persons' inability to believe. Paradoxically, those who reject Christ will believe almost anything else—reincarnation, astrology, Oriental religions, humanist philosophy, atheism, or drugs as the key to meaningful life. There are those among us today who believe in Satan and worship him but refuse to believe in Christ!

The only answer I have been able to give for the often-violent rejection of the Christian faith is that the world in its carnality hates the demand of Jesus Christ that human beings live pure and holy lives. So it continues to cry for peace on earth, when the Prince of peace is the only One who can bring lasting peace. It cries for justice and better distribution of the world's wealth, but it refuses to recognize that there will always be greed, lack of concern for others, and cruelty until the human heart is changed. Only Jesus can do that.

The world wants all the things that only Jesus can provide, but it is unwilling to pay the price of surrendering to Christ so that the carnal, immoral nature can be put to death.

Jesus warned, "All men will hate you because of me" (Matt. 10:22), and, "In the world ye shall have tribulation" (John 16:33, KJV), but He immediately added, "but be of good cheer; I have overcome the world."

Titus 2:11-12 tells us how we should live in the midst of a carnal, evil world: "The grace of God . . . teaches us to say 'No' to ungodliness and worldly passions, and to live self-controlled, upright and godly lives in this present age."

The influence of the new morality on the church has been nowhere more embarrassingly apparent in recent years than in the area of sexual morality. The media has had a field day exposing TV evangelists and other well-known ministers and Christian leaders whose private lives were quite different from their public images. And for every "famous" personality who receives front-page attention, churches large and small all across the country are having to deal with the moral misconduct of their pastors and other staff people, though without the glare of media publicity.

The Christian community has been reeling from the shock of every new exposure and asks, "Who is next?" Church members look at their ministers with suspicious glances and wonder if they also are guilty of leading a double life. A recent poll among the clergy revealed that 23 percent admitted sexually inappropriate behavior since being in a local church ministry. Twelve percent admitted to sexual intercourse with someone other than their spouses since being in a local church ministry. The unbelieving world is delighted and reinforced in its belief that all of us are phonies because of the misconduct of some.

Nothing has hurt the cause of Christ in the 2,000 years of the church era more than the moral scandals that have rocked the Christian world in recent years. Because moral failures in the Christian community are reaching epidemic proportions and because of the damage they are creating for our witness for Christ, we need a strong reminder of what the biblical teachings on morality are.

We need to examine carefully the biblical teachings on sexual morality to determine what God's requirements actually are, and we need to be reminded of the consequences if we disobey them. In the following pages I have made a careful collection of what the Old Testaments says about sexual immorality and its specific commands in this area. I have done the same thing for the New Testament. I believe that the overwhelming evidence will support my insistence that sexual immorality is one of the major causes, if not *the* major cause, of the unhappiness that grips so many people. Will we never learn that we cannot successfully break God's commands without breaking ourselves?

What the Old Testament Says about Sexual Immorality

1. As beings created in the image and likeness of God, we should be holy as He is holy (Gen. 1:26; see Lev. 19:2).
2. Man and woman were ordained to be united and become one. God's original will was that this union not be broken except by death (Gen. 2:24; Mal. 2:11-16).
3. Though the interpretation is debated, Genesis 6:1-7 seems to suggest that sexual immorality was at the root of God's decree to destroy the earth by water.
4. Sexual immorality was involved in God's decree to destroy Sodom and Gomorrah (Gen. 18:20; 19:4-9; see Jude 7).
5. It would have been a sin against God if Abimelech had had sexual relations with Sarah (Gen. 20:6).

6. Shechem's sexual relation with Dinah outside marriage is called "a disgraceful thing . . . a thing that should not be done" (Gen. 34:7).

7. Onan's deed is called "wicked in the Lord's sight" (Gen. 38:9-10).

8. Joseph said that yielding to the enticements of Potiphar's wife would have been "sin against God" (Gen. 39:9).

9. Reuben was rebuked for sleeping with his father's concubine (Gen. 49:4; see 35:22).

10. When making a covenant with Israel at Mount Sinai, God said they were to be "a holy nation" (Ex. 19:6; Lev. 19:2; and Deut. 26:19).

11. Homosexuality is called "vile" . . . "disgraceful" (Judg. 19:22-24; see Judg. 20:4-11).

12. Eli's house was to be punished because of the sexual immorality of his sons and his failures to restrain them (1 Sam. 2:22-25; 3:12-14).

13. David's adultery was rebuked by Nathan, and punishment came to him (2 Sam. 11—12).

14. Amnon's rape of his half sister resulted in his murder by Absalom (2 Sam. 13:1-35) and was a factor in Absalom's revolt against David (2 Sam. 13—15).

15. In defense of his righteousness, Job said he did not look lustfully at a girl or have adulterous relations (Job 31:1). Job 31:9-12 called adultery "a fire that burns to Destruction."

16. Participation in cultic male prostitution brings punishment (Job 36:13-14).

17. Those who worship God must have a "pure heart" (Ps. 24:3-4; see Ps. 73:1).

18 Adultery is condemned and should be avoided; it will be punished (Ps. 50:18,21; see Prov. 2:16-19; 5:1-14,20; 6:23-35; 7:5-27; 30:20; Isa. 57:3-8; Jer. 5:7-9; 7:9-11; Ezek. 18:11,13,15,17; 22:10-11; and Hos. 1—3; 4:13-15).

19. A young man can keep his way pure by living according to God's Word (Ps. 119:9; see Prov. 20:9; 22:11).

20. The prostitute is to be avoided, and prostitution is condemned (Prov. 7:26; 23:26-28; 31:3; see Isa. 23:15-18; 57:3-8; Jer. 5:7-9; Hos. 4:10-11,13-15; Joel 3:3; Amos 2:7; Mic. 1:7; and Nah. 3:4).

21. The prophets frequently used adultery and prostitution as analogies for Israel's faithfulness to God. In some passages it is uncertain whether the adultery/prostitution is figurative for faithlessness to God or literal (Jer. 3:1-3,6-10,20; 5:7-9; 13:27; Ezek. 16; 23; 24:13; Hos. 1—3; 4:10-12,13-15; 5:3-4; 6:10; 7:4; 9:1; and Nah. 3:4).
22. Incest is condemned (Ezek. 22:10-11).
23. Voyeurism is condemned (Hab. 2:15).

Old Testament Commands Regarding Sexual Immorality

I have separated statements regarding sexual immorality from specific commands, though by implication the statements listed above require obedience. It is surprising how few specific commands are found in the Old Testament regarding sexual immorality.

1. Adultery was emphatically prohibited (Ex. 20:14; see Lev. 18:20; 20:10; and Deut. 5:18; 22:22).
2. The man who seduced a virgin was required to marry her or pay the bridal price whether or not her father permitted them to marry (Ex. 22:16-17; Deut. 22:28-29). He was to be put to death if she was already engaged (Deut. 22:25-27). Both of them were to be put to death if he lay with her in the city and she did not cry for help (Deut. 22:23-24).
3. In the case of adultery, both the man and woman were to be put to death (Deut. 22:22).
4. Those who had sexual relations with animals were to be put to death (Ex. 22:19; see Lev. 18:23; 20:15-16).
5. No one was to have sexual relations with family members (prohibition of incest: Lev. 18:6-18,29; 20:11-12,14,17,19-21; and Deut. 22:30).
6. A man was not to have sexual relations with another man (Lev. 18:22,29; 20:13).
7. Daughters were not to be made prostitutes (Lev. 19:29; 21:9; or sons, Deut. 23:17-18).
8. Priests were not to marry prostitutes (Lev. 21:13-15).
9. A wife suspected of adultery had to submit to a test to prove her innocence (Num. 5:11-31).
10. A woman was to be a virgin when she married (Deut. 22:13-21).

11. The genitals were not to be seized by a wife helping her husband in a fight with another man (Deut. 25:11-12).

12. To the pure God's people were to show themselves pure (2 Sam. 22:27).

    In summary, God's people were commanded to be holy as God is holy (Lev. 19:2).

What the New Testament Says About Sexual Immorality

The New Testament is much more concerned with sexual immorality than the Old Testament as evidenced by the number of comments on the subject.

1. Those who are pure in heart are happy, for they will see God (Matt. 5:8).

2. Anyone who looks at a woman lustfully has already committed adultery with her in his heart (Matt. 5:27-28).

3. Divorce and adultery cannot be separated (Matt. 5:32; 19:8-9; and Rom. 7:1-3).

4. Man and woman were ordained to be united and become one. God's original will was that this union not be broken except by death (Matt. 14:4; see Matt. 19:1-9; Mark 6:18; 10:1-12; and 1 Cor. 7:10-14,39).

5. Sexual immorality (fornication, KJV) and adultery are among the evils that come from within and make a person unclean (Mark 7:20-23).

6. Small and narrow is the way that leads to life; wide is the gate and broad the way that leads to destruction (Matt. 7:13-14; see Luke 13:24).

7. Jesus does not approve of adultery but offers forgiveness for the one who has committed this sin (John 8:2-11).

8. Early Gentile Christians were exhorted to abstain from sexual immorality (fornication, KJV; Acts 15:20,29; 21:25).

9. Those who do not know God or glorify Him are given over to the sinful desires of their hearts, including sexual impurity, lust (vile affections, KJV), homosexuality, and depraved minds (Rom. 1:21-32).

10. We are warned against committing adultery (Rom. 2:22) and sexual immorality (fornication, KJV; see 1 Cor. 6:18; 10:8; and Heb.

12:16).

11. Living according to the sinful nature and its desires cannot please God and leads to death, but the mind controlled by the Spirit is life and peace (Rom. 8:5-8).

12. Sexual immorality on the part of any member of the body should bring grief to the entire body (1 Cor. 5:1-2).

13. A person committing incest should be excluded from Christian fellowship (an interpretation of "hand this man over to Satan," 1 Cor. 5:1-5,9-11).

14. Christian fellowship should be withheld from a brother who is sexually immoral (a fornicator, KJV; 1 Cor. 5:11).

15. The sexually immoral (fornicators, KJV), adulterers, male prostitutes, and homosexual offenders (effeminate and abusers of themselves with mankind, KJV) will not inherit the kingdom of God (1 Cor. 6:9-10), but even these sins can be forgiven and cleansed by Jesus (1 Cor. 6:11; see Eph. 5:5).

16. Because we are united with Christ and our bodies are the temple of the Holy Spirit, we should flee sexual immorality (fornication, KJV) or union with a prostitute (1 Cor. 6:12-20).

17. When we sin sexually (committeth fornication, KJV), we sin against our own body (1 Cor. 6:18).

18. To avoid sexual immorality, men and women should marry and find their sexual gratification only within marriage (1 Cor. 7:2-6,9).

19. Purity should be an attribute of a servant of God (2 Cor. 6:6).

20. We should purify ourselves from everything that contaminates body and spirit (2 Cor. 7:1; see 1 John 3:3).

21. We grieve other Christians when we do not repent of the impurity, sexual sin, and debauchery in which we may have indulged (2 Cor. 12:21).

22. If we live by the Spirit, we will not gratify the desires of the sinful nature, which include the following: sexual immorality, impurity, and debauchery (Gal. 5:16,19; see 1 Pet. 4:1-4).

23. Those who belong to Christ have crucified the sinful nature (flesh, KJV) with its passions and desires (Gal. 5:24).

24. Those who sow to please the sinful nature from the nature will reap destruction (Gal. 6:8).

25. Those who are dead in their transgressions and sins gratify the cravings of the sinful nature and follow its desires and thoughts (Eph. 2:1-3; see Eph. 4:19).

26. Even a hint of sexual immorality or of any kind of impurity is improper for God's holy people (Eph. 5:3).

27. We should let our thoughts dwell on things that are true, noble, right, pure, lovely, admirable, excellent, or praiseworthy (Phil. 4:8; see Col. 3:2).

28. It is God's will that we should avoid sexual immorality (fornication, KJV) in order to control our body in a way that is holy and honorable (1 Thess. 4:3-5; see Rev. 2:14,20).

29. God did not call us to be impure (uncleanness, KJV) but to live a holy life (1 Thess. 4:7; see 2 Pet. 3:11,14).

30. The law was made for lawbreakers, rebels, the ungodly, sinful, unholy and irreligious, murderers, adulterers, perverts, etc., all of which are contrary to the sound doctrine that conforms to the glorious gospel of God (1 Tim. 1:9-11).

31. We should live quiet lives in all godliness and holiness (1 Tim. 2:2).

32. Women should dress modestly and with decency and propriety (1 Tim. 2:9).

33. We should be examples for other believers in speech, life, love, faith, and purity (1 Tim. 4:12).

34. The grace of God that brings salvation teaches us to say no to ungodliness and worldly passions (worldly lusts, KJV) and to live self-controlled, upright, and godly lives (Titus 2:11-12; see 1 Pet. 1:13-15).

35. The high priest who meets our needs is holy, blameless, and pure (Heb. 7:26).

36. God will judge the adulterer and all the sexually immoral (Heb. 13:4; see 1 Pet. 4:1-5; 2 Pet. 2:4-17; and Rev. 21:8).

37. We should get rid of all moral filth (Jas. 1:21).

38. Some prayers are not answered because they come from wrong motives to spend what is received on pleasures (Jas. 4:3).

39. We should abstain from sinful desires (fleshly lusts, KJV), which war against the soul (1 Pet. 2:11).

40. Unbelievers will heap abuse on us for not joining them in de

bauchery, lust, and an excess of dissipation (1 Pet. 4:3-4).

41. Those who follow the corrupt desire of the sinful nature (walk after the flesh in the lust of uncleanness, KJV) carouse openly, commit adultery, never stop sinning, seduce the unstable, etc., but blackest darkness is reserved for them (2 Pet. 2:10-17).

42. The wicked appeal to the lustful desires of sinful human nature, entice people who are just escaping from those who live in error, promise them freedom, though they themselves are slaves of depravity (2 Pet. 2:18-19).

43. Everything in the world—the cravings of sinful man (the lust of the flesh, KJV), the lust of the eyes, and the boasting of what we do and have—come not from God but from the world (1 John 2:16).

44. Nothing impure (that defiles, KJV) or sexually immoral (whoremongers, KJV) will enter the new Jerusalem (Rev. 21:27; 22:15).

New Testament Commands Regarding Sexual Immorality

The commands listed below have been limited only to those verses that are expressed in the imperative form of the verb in the Greek language. It could well be argued that many of the previously enumerated statements about sexual immorality found in the New Testament imply that they are commands to be obeyed.

1. "Do not let sin reign in your mortal body . . . Do not offer the parts of your body to sin" (Rom. 6:12-14).

2. Offer the parts of your body in slavery to righteousness leading to holiness (Rom. 6:19-23; see Rom. 12:1).

3. The Old Testament command against adultery is reaffirmed in the New Testament (Rom. 13:9; see Matt. 5:27-28; 19:18; Mark 10:19; and Jas. 2:11).

4. We are commanded to love our neighbor; if we do, we will not commit adultery or wrong him in any way (Rom. 13:9-10).

5. We are to behave decently, not participating in orgies, sexual immorality, and debauchery. We are to clothe ourselves with Jesus Christ and not think about how to gratify the desires of the sinful nature (Rom. 13:13-14).

6. We are to flee from sexual immorality (fornication, KJV; 1 Cor. 6:18; see 1 Cor. 10:8).

7. Christians are not to seek a divorce (1 Cor. 7:10-16).
8. We are to set our minds on things above, not on earthly things (Col. 3:2).
9. We are to put to death whatever belongs to the earthly nature, such as sexual immorality, impurity, lust, and evil desires (Col. 3:5).
10. We are to flee the evil desire of youth (youthful lusts, KJV; 2 Tim. 2:22).
11. We are commanded to purify our hearts (Jas. 4:8).

Conclusion

This examination of passages in the Old and New Testaments that deal with the subject of sexual immorality leads to the following conclusions:

1. The New Testament says more about sexual immorality than the Old Testament (though the New Testament occupies only one-fifth of the total content of the Bible).
2. There are surprisingly few specific commands in either the Old or New Testament regarding sexual immorality, although there are many warnings and exhortations.
3. Both the Old and New Testaments are in agreement in their condemnation of sexual immorality.

Living according to biblical moral principles is not an option for Christians. It is an absolute imperative, not only for our personal happiness and well-being but also because it serves as perhaps the single, most effective witness to the claim we make before a lost world that Christ transforms life and truly makes us different.

Principle: True obedience requires that we obey the moral commands of God.

Note

1. Genesis 3:5. I intentionally said, "become God" instead of what most theologians would say: "become like God." Humankind's desire has not been to become like God— holy, pure, righteous, and self-sacrificing—but to take the place of God and establish our own standards of what is acceptable moral conduct.

12
Biblical Teachings on Obedience

A cursory examination of the words *obey/obedience* and *command/commandment* in a Bible concordance serves as an impressive reminder of the biblical emphasis on obedience. Without considering the Old Testament passages on obedience, the New Testament reveals a great deal about its importance.

What the New Testament Reveals About Obedience

Without any attempt to be exhaustive, I have listed some of the New Testament teachings about obedience. They include the following:

1. We are to obey the commands in order to enter life (Matt. 19:17).
2. We are to teach new disciples to obey Christ's commands (Matt. 28:20).
3. Even evil spirits obey Christ when He gives orders to them (Mark 1:27).
4. Jesus was obedient to His earthly parents (Luke 2:51).
5. Blessed are those who hear and obey the Word of God (Luke 11:28).
6. The commands of God lead to eternal life (John 12:50).
7. Jesus commands us to love one another (John 13:34-35; 15:12,17; 1 Pet. 1:22; 4:8; 2 Pet. 1:7; and 1 John 3:23; 4:7,21).
8. If we love Christ, we will obey His commands and teachings (John 14:15,23-24).
9. Those who do not love Christ will not obey His teachings (John 14:24).
10. Those who obey the commands prove that they truly love Jesus (John 14:21,23).

11. We remain in Christ's love if we obey His commands (John 15:10).

12. We are Christ's friends if we do what He commands (John 15:14).

13. Those who are Christ's obey God's Word (John 17:6).

14. We must obey God rather than men (Acts 4:19-20; 5:29).

15. The Holy Spirit is given by God to those who obey Him (Acts 5:32).

16. People are called to the obedience that comes from faith (Rom. 1:5).

17. Those who obey are declared righteous in God's sight (Rom. 2:13).

18. Grace and the gift of righteousness come through the obedience of one person: Jesus Christ (Rom. 5:17-19).

19. The obedience of Christ makes many righteous (Rom. 5:19).

20. We are not to obey the evil desires of the mortal body (Rom. 6:12).

21. Obedience leads to righteousness (Rom. 6:16).

22. People everywhere will hear about obedient Christians (Rom. 16:19).

23. Through the proclamation of the gospel all nations may believe and obey Jesus Christ (Rom. 16:25-26).

24. The Lord has commanded that those who preach the gospel should receive their living from it (1 Cor. 9:14).

25. People will praise God for the obedience that accompanies the confession of the gospel of Christ (2 Cor. 9:13).

26. We should bring every thought into obedience to Christ (2 Cor. 10:5).

27. The entire law is summed up in a single command: "Love your neighbor as yourself" (Gal. 5:14).

28. It is right to obey parents (Eph. 6:1; Col. 3:20; and 1 Tim. 3:4).

29. It is right to obey those who exercise authority over us (Eph. 6:5; Col. 3:22; Heb. 13:17; and 1 Pet. 2:13-14).

30. Obedience to earthly masters should be with sincerity of heart (Eph. 6:5; see 1 Pet. 2:18).

31. Obedience requires humbling of self (Phil. 2:8).

32. Christ was obedient unto death (Phil. 2:8).

33. It is pleasing to God to obey parents (Col. 3:20).

34. Punishment awaits those who do not obey the gospel of Christ (2 Thess. 1:8; 1 Pet. 4:17).
35. Obedience may be learned through suffering (Heb. 5:8).
36. Jesus is the source of eternal salvation for all who obey Him (Heb. 5:9).
37. Because of his faith Abraham obeyed God (Heb. 11:8).
38. The elect are chosen for obedience to Christ (1 Pet. 1:2).
39. If we are obedient, we will not conform to the evil desires we had before being saved (1 Pet. 1:14).
40. If we obey the truth, we will purify ourselves (1 Pet. 1:22).
41. Sincere love for other Christians is linked to obeying the truth (1 Pet. 1:22).
42. Obeying Christ's commands is an assurance that we know Christ (1 John 2:3,6).
43. If we obey Christ's word, God's love is truly made complete in us (1 John 2:5).
44. Obedience is a factor in receiving answers to prayers (1 John 3:22).
45. Those who obey Christ's commands live in Him and He in them (1 John 3:24).
46. We know that we love the children of God by obeying God's commands (1 John 5:2).
47. Love for God is to obey His commands (1 John 5:3; 2 John 6).
48. God's commands are not burdensome (1 John 5:3).
49. We are commanded to walk in love (2 John 6).
50. We are to obey what we have received and heard (Rev. 3:3).

Specific Commands in the New Testament

The Old Testament rabbis found 613 laws in the Mosaic law code. I have not attempted to make a list of every command found in the New Testament as it would require an examination of every imperative form in the Greek New Testament to determine which ones are commands for Christians. Some of the commands (not suggestions) found in the New Testament include the following:

1. We are commanded to let our light shine before men (Matt. 5:16).
2. We are commanded to be reconciled to our brothers (Matt. 5:23-24).

3. We are commanded not to swear (Matt. 5:34-37; Jas. 5:12).

4. We are commanded not to resist an evil person (Matt. 5:39).

5. We are commanded to love our enemies (Matt. 5:44; Luke 6:27).

6. We are commanded not to make a display of prayer (Matt. 6:5-8).

7. We are commanded to store up treasures in heaven, not on earth (Matt. 6:19-20).

8. We are commanded not to be anxious about the necessities of life (Matt. 6:25; Luke 12:22).

9. We are commanded not to judge others (Matt. 7:1; Luke 6:37; and Rom. 14:13).

10. We are commanded to watch out for false prophets (Matt. 7:15).

11. We are commanded to do to others what we would have them do to us (Matt. 7:12).

12. We are commanded to be watchful for the end (Matt. 25:13; Mark 13:33; and Luke 12:40).

13. We are commanded to go and make disciples and to teach them to obey Christ's commands (Matt. 28:19-20; Mark 16:15).

14. We are commanded to love God and our neighbor (Mark 12:30-31).

15. We are commanded to be generous (Luke 6:38).

16. We are commanded to love one another (John 13:34-35; 15:12,17).

17. We are commanded not to be conformed to the world (Rom. 12:2).

18. We are commanded not to think of ourselves more highly than we ought (Rom. 12:3).

19. We are commanded to hate evil and love good (Rom. 12:9).

20. We are commanded to honor others above ourselves (Rom. 12:10; see Phil. 2:3).

21. We are commanded to share with those in need (Rom. 12:13).

22. We are commanded not to repay anyone evil for evil (Rom. 12:17; 1 Pet. 3:9).

23. We are commanded to flee from sexual immorality (1 Cor. 6:18; put it to death, Col. 3:5).

24. We are commanded not to cause others to stumble (1 Cor. 10:32).

25. We are commanded not to be yoked together with unbelievers (2 Cor. 6:14).

26. We are commanded not to use our freedom to indulge the sinful nature (Gal. 5:13).
27. We are commanded to speak truthfully (Eph. 4:25; Col. 3:9).
28. We are commanded not to speak unwholesome words (Eph. 4:29; 5:4).
29. We are commanded not to grieve the Holy Spirit (Eph. 4:30).
30. We are commanded to be kind, compassionate, and forgiving (Eph. 4:32; Col. 3:12-13).
31. We are commanded to be filled with the Spirit (Eph. 5:18).
32. We are commanded to observe duties in the relationship of husband, wife, child, or parent (Eph. 5:22—6:4; Col. 3:18-21; and 1 Pet. 3:1-7).
33. We are commanded not to act out of ambition or conceit (Phil. 2:3).
34. We are commanded not to complain or argue (Phil. 2:14; Jas. 5:9).
35. We are commanded to rejoice in the Lord (Phil. 3:1; 1 Thess. 5:16).
36. We are commanded to guard our thoughts (Phil. 4:8; Col. 3:2).
37. We are commanded to avoid sexual immorality (1 Thess. 4:3; 1 Pet. 2:11).
38. We are commanded to pray continually (1 Thess. 5:17).
39. We are commanded to give thanks in all circumstances (1 Thess. 5:18).
40. We are commanded to keep away from those brothers who are idle and who do not live according to the biblical teachings (2 Thess. 3:6).
41. We are commanded not to be idle or busybodies (2 Thess. 3:11-12).
42. We are commanded never to tire of doing what is right (2 Thess. 3:13).
43. We are commanded to keep ourselves pure (1 Tim. 5:22).
44. The rich are commanded not to be arrogant or to put their hope in wealth (1 Tim. 6:17).
45. We are commanded not to show favoritism (Jas. 2:1-9).
46. We are commanded to submit to God (Jas. 4:7).
47. We are commanded not to slander one another (Jas. 4:11; 1 Pet.

2:1).

48. We are commanded to pray for the sick (Jas. 5:13-16).
49. We are commanded to rid ourselves of malice, deceit, hypocrisy, envy, and slander (1 Pet. 2:1).
50. We are commanded to believe in the name of God's son, Jesus Christ (1 John 3:23).
51. We are commanded to walk in the truth (2 John 4).
52. We are commanded to worship God! (Rev. 22:9).

Can One Obedient Person Make a Difference?

What kind of world would we live in if every command in the Scriptures were conscientiously observed by every person? If this happened, we would have to change the name of our planet from "Earth" to "Heaven." Whatever else heaven may be, it will be a place characterized by total obedience to God, for there will be no disobedience of even a thought or desire in heaven. Can you imagine what that will be like? It will be a place where there will be no lying, cheating, stealing, immorality, killing, violence, oppression, or mistreatment of any kind. It is not surprising that the apostle Paul could long to be there: "For to me, to live is Christ and to die is gain" (Phil. 1:21).

Do we have to wait to cross to the other side to experience what heaven will be like? Each of us who makes commitment to total obedience brings a little taste of heaven to earth for ourselves and for those around us. By our obedience to Christ, we become visual signposts for others to point them the way to true happiness.

Happiness will not be found by disobeying God. It never has been found that way. Disobedience to God's command did not bring happiness to the first man and woman who believed the lie that disobedience was a shortcut to finding happiness. Obedience to God was and remains the key to happiness. This foundational principle was established at the beginning of human history and has never been rescinded.

No one can be forced to obey God, though He could overpower us and give us no other option if He chose. If God does not use His power to require obedience, then we cannot force anyone else to obey the rule of God through Christ. However, we can be responsible for our own small corner in the world to bring light to those whose paths intersect ours.

Obedience is the willingness to do whatever God asks us to do at any given moment, however foolish, dangerous, or self-sacrificing it may appear. "No discipline seems pleasant at the time, but painful. Later on, however, it produces a harvest of righteousness and peace for those who have been trained by it" (Heb. 12:11). And it could be added, the discipline of obedience produces happiness as nothing else can.

Can one person make a difference? To answer that question let me tell you about Keith. I met Keith, a recent convert, at a church where I was leading a Bible study. He told me the story of how one obedient Christian can make an impact on those around him like the concentric circles produced when a pebble is tossed in water. Two weeks after becoming a Christian, and not yet out of his teens, Keith was inducted into the navy and sent to boot camp in San Diego. His friends were much concerned that as a new Christian Keith would not have the inner resources to resist the temptations he would encounter as a young man away from home for the first time. But they were wrong.

The first night in the large barracks room that contained forty-eight bunks, just before the lights were turned out, Keith felt a strong urge to kneel beside his bunk to pray. However, thoughts of the ridicule the others would heap on him terrified him, so he crawled into the bunk without praying but hardly slept that night.

The next night Keith felt the same urge, but, not wanting to experience another sleepless night, he knelt beside his bunk and prayed. He held his breath, waiting for catcalls or for shoes to be thrown at him, but nothing happened. The next night, more emboldened, Keith again knelt beside his bunk to pray. That night one other sailor joined him. By the end of the first week five young sailors were kneeling beside their bunks to pray just before the lights were turned out.

By the end of that first month all forty-eight men in that barracks were kneeling beside their bunks to pray before the lights went out! Eight of them, already Christians, rededicated their lives to God, and seven others were converted. All this came about because of the courageous obedience of one new convert who did not know better than to obey the impulse God had planted in his heart to kneel beside his bunk and pray openly, regardless of the ridicule he might experience.

A candle-lighting service in a darkened church sanctuary is a never-to-be-forgotten experience. Each participant is given a candle upon entering and told to light it at a given signal. The first lighted candle seems overwhelmed by the darkness, but as candle after candle is lit, the room begins to be bathed in a glow of light until, finally, the darkest corner of the sanctuary is clearly visible. One candle alone does not dispel the darkness, but together the candles become a bright light. Each is important; together they transform the darkness.

We are like those candles—separately we may feel we make no difference, yet each of us is a necessary component of the total witness. Together we bring a bright light to the darkness of our world if we are obedient.

Principle: Obedience to God is the key to finding happiness. Happy are those who obey God, for they are the ones who one day will hear, "Well done, good and faithful servant."